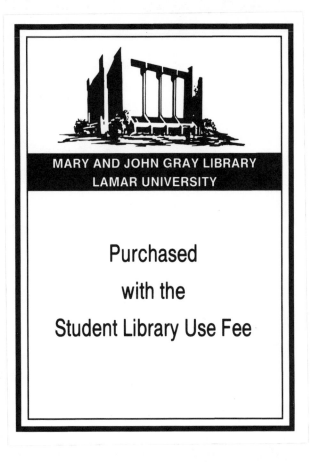

THE WORLD IS ROUND JUST LIKE AN ORANGE

DISCARDED

MANY WAYS OF LEARNING

TITLES IN THIS SET

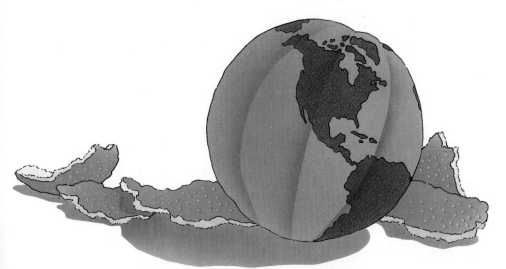

Acknowledgments appear on page 144.

345678910RRS99989796959493

THE WORLD IS
ROUND
JUST LIKE
AN ORANGE

MANY WAYS OF LEARNING

ScottForesman
A Division of HarperCollinsPublishers

CONTENTS

I CAN DO IT!

STUDENT RESOURCES

THE

IMPERFECT/PERFECT

BOOK REPORT

by Johanna Hurwitz

There was no doubt about it. Zoe Mitchell was just as smart as Cricket Kaufman. Everyone who had known Cricket since she had been the star of the morning kindergarten class, back when she was five years old, agreed. Finally, she had met her match.

In some ways, it made Cricket feel strange not to be the best student in the class. But at the same time, she worked harder than ever and found that she liked school better and better. She was learning so many new things. It was hard to decide if it was because now she was in fourth grade or because she was working not to let Zoe get ahead of her. Lucas Cott was smart too, but it wasn't the same thing. Maybe it was because he was the smartest boy in the class and she had been the smartest girl. Now, whenever test papers were handed back, Cricket craned her head to see what mark Zoe had gotten. Almost always, the two girls had performed equally well.

Mrs. Schraalenburgh beamed proudly at them both when they each got 100 percent on the fractions test in arithmetic. But she also congratulated Julio for improving his score. When Cricket walked to the back of the room to use the pencil sharpener, she was able to see that Julio had almost as many problems wrong as he had gotten right. Mrs. Schraalenburgh was a funny teacher. She always said she was proud of all her students and to prove it she never singled one person out above the others. Maybe that was why it wasn't quite so bad that Zoe Mitchell was such a good student. If Cricket wasn't the teacher's pet this year, neither was Zoe. No one was. With a different "personality of the day" selected each morning, and students like Julio being congratulated even when they could only answer half the questions, everyone was treated equally.

Still, when Mrs. Schraalenburgh said that once a month everyone had to write a book report, Cricket was delighted. She loved reading and a book report would be fun for her to write. She would do one that was so much better than everyone else's that Mrs. Schraalenburgh would have to admit that she was the very best student in the class. Although Cricket was pleased with the new assignment, there were loud groans from the back of the room.

"Quiet!" Mrs. Schraalenburgh scolded. "If you have something to say, raise your hands and I will call on you." She looked at Lucas, who had made the loudest groan.

"Don't you like to read, Lucas?" asked the teacher.

"Sure," said Lucas. "But I don't like writing book reports."

"A book report is a way of sharing something that you have enjoyed with the rest of the class," said Mrs. Schraalenburgh. "It should tell your classmates whether or not they too should read that book."

I M P E R F E C T

Lucas did not look convinced. Cricket knew he read a lot of books. She saw him checking them out of the school library when the class had library time. But she also knew he was lazy about doing homework. She, on the other hand, couldn't wait to begin. She would make the best book report that anyone ever did. Then, perhaps finally, Mrs. Schraalenburgh would know what a great student she was.

Cricket had read so many books since the school year had begun that at first she couldn't make up her mind which to use for her report. Finally, she decided to write her report on the book that she had given to Zoe. It was *Dear Mr. Henshaw* by Beverly Clearly. It was too bad she couldn't find a copy of it in the library. But Cricket remembered the story very well, and she thought she could write a report from her memory. Her memory was very good and it had been only a couple of weeks since she had read the book.

Cricket sat down and wrote, covering both sides of a sheet of loose-leaf paper as she told all about the book. Then, very neatly, she copied it over. She used a razor-edged marking pen that she had bought with her allowance last week. The

P E R F E C T

letters came out clear and neat, but near the
bottom of the page, she made a mistake. Cricket
didn't want to have any crossing-out on her
report. So she took a fresh piece of paper and
copied her report over again, very slowly this
time so that she wouldn't make another error.
When she was finished, it looked beautiful. It was
the neatest piece of homework that she had ever
done.

Then, to enhance the report, she decided to
make a special cover for it. She took two sheets
of red-colored paper. With her pencil and a ruler,
she drew lines across the top of the page. She did
it very, very lightly so that afterward she would
be able to erase the lines. Then, using the block
letters that they had been learning to do in art
class, she wrote the title and the author.

Dear Mr. Henshaw, by Beverly Clearly.
Book Report by Cricket Kaufman.

Underneath, she drew a picture of a boy sitting at
a desk and writing. People who hadn't read the
book might think it was supposed to be a picture
of Cricket writing her book report, but if you read
the book or at least read Cricket's report about it,
you would know that it was supposed to be Leigh

Botts, the main character in the story. He was always writing letters to his favorite author, who was named Mr. Henshaw. Cricket colored in the picture with her markers, and she erased the lines from the top of the paper.

Cricket had her own stapler. She used it to staple the top cover and the back cover to the page with her report. When she was finally finished, it was time for bed. She had missed her favorite Thursday evening television program. But she was so proud of her completed book report that she didn't even mind. Wait until Mrs. Schraalenburgh sees my wonderful report, she thought. She knew that the teacher would have to be very impressed with her careful work.

The next morning Cricket proudly handed in her report.

"You didn't tell us we had to make covers," said Connie Alf when she saw Cricket's masterpiece.

"We didn't have to make covers," said Julio. Cricket looked at the paper he was putting on the teacher's desk. Wait until Mrs. Schraalenburgh saw that he had written a report about *Mr. Popper's Penguins,* which she read to them at the beginning of September. It was cheating to write

IMPERFECT

a report about a book that you hadn't even read. Listening didn't count. And besides, everyone in the class already knew about the story. Julio will be in big trouble, Cricket decided.

"I wrote about the book that you gave me," Zoe whispered to Cricket as she put hers in the pile. "It was a great book and it was fun to write about it." She smiled at Cricket. But Cricket did not smile back. It hadn't occurred to her that Zoe would use the same book that she did for her report.

"How long was your report?" Cricket asked her.

"It was all one side and a little bit of the other side of the paper," said Zoe.

Cricket began to feel better. Her report was longer and her report had a fancy cover. Her report had to be a lot better than Zoe's. In fact, having another report on the same book to compare with hers would make Mrs. Schraalenburgh realize all the more how much effort Cricket had put into the assignment. She smiled at Zoe. It was a good thing that they had both written about the same book, after all.

Mrs. Schraalenburgh took all the reports and put them inside her canvas tote bag. "I'll take these home to read over the weekend," she

PERFECT

promised. "On Monday, I'll give them back and we'll share them together."

All weekend Cricket glowed inside as she thought about her wonderful book report. She just knew that her teacher was going to love it. She couldn't wait until they were returned on Monday. Mrs. Schraalenburgh would probably write on the report how fabulous it was.

The reports were not returned to the students until after lunch on Monday. Cricket could hardly sit still as the teacher walked about the room handing them back. She decided that she would try and keep a straight face. It would be hard not to grin from ear to ear when she was reading the teacher's comments. But on the other hand, it would look as if she were showing off when other students such as Julio got bad marks on their reports. She held her breath as Mrs. Schraalenburgh stood at her desk and sorted through the remaining papers in her hand.

"Here's yours, Cricket," said the teacher. She patted Cricket on the back. "I'm sure you'll do better next time, so don't worry too much about your grade."

Cricket couldn't imagine what the teacher was referring to. There was nothing written on

the red cover of her report, but when she opened it up, she saw a B− written on the top of the page. Cricket couldn't believe it. How could she possibly have gotten such a low mark? This was an A+ report. It didn't make sense. Then Cricket noticed that on the inside of the back cover, Mrs. Schraalenburgh had written a message.

It is careless of you to misspell the name of the author whom you are writing about. The author of this book spells her last name CLEARY. Also, the award that this book won is called the NEWBERY Medal, not NEWBERRY. If you read your report over, you will see that you said the same thing three different times. It is better to say what you have to once and not bore your readers. I am glad you liked this book and I am sure next time you will write a better report to prove it.

Cricket's eyes blurred with tears. She couldn't believe it. Mrs. Schraalenburgh didn't like her report. So what if she had spelled the author's name wrong? What did it matter? She had never said that spelling was going to count in their book reports.

"I am going to have a few people read their reports out loud to share them with us now," said Mrs. Schraalenburgh. "Let's start with Julio," she said.

Cricket blinked back her tears. If she had gotten a B−, Julio must have gotten a D.

"I gave Julio an A for his report," the teacher said as Julio walked proudly up to the front of the room.

"Even though Julio wrote about a book that we have already read and talked about in class this year, he has captured the humor of the story and what he has to say about the book will make anyone who hasn't already read it want to read it," she said.

Julio cleared his throat and waited until he had everyone's attention. Then he read his report. It was short, Cricket noted. But he made everyone laugh when he reminded them of one of the funny scenes in the book.

"Suppose you wrote about a book you didn't like," said Connie.

"Why would you bother to do that?" asked Mrs. Schraalenburgh. "If you didn't like the book, you should have stopped reading it and looked for another one."

I M P E R F E C T

All the children looked at each other. They had never heard a teacher say that you should stop reading a book.

"Do you know how many books are in the school library?" Mrs. Schraalenburgh asked.

"One hundred," guessed Julio.

Cricket raised her hand. She had once asked the librarian, so she knew the correct answer.

"Many, many more than a hundred," said Mrs. Schraalenburgh.

"Two hundred," someone called out.

"No speaking out," Mrs. Schraalenburgh reminded the students. "Cricket, do you know?" asked the teacher.

"Eight thousand," she said.

There were loud gasps. Eight thousand was a big number.

"That's right," said Mrs. Schraalenburgh. "And don't you think that if there are eight thousand books right here in this school building you could find one that you would like? So why would you waste your time reading a book you don't like?"

"But if we have to make book reports every month from now on, we'll need to find more than *one* book," Lucas pointed out.

PERFECT

"That's right," Connie agreed.

"I suspect that if you gave it a try, you could find many, many books that you will like among the eight thousand books in the school library. And what about the public library? Do you know how many books they have there?"

"Eight thousand," someone guessed.

Mrs. Schraalenburgh shook her head. "The next time you go, ask the children's librarian how many books are in the collection there," she said.

"And next time, Julio will write about a new book. One that he hasn't read or heard read to him before," Mrs. Schraalenburgh added. "Right, Julio?"

Julio grinned at the teacher. "Right," he said. "I want to see if I can make an A every time."

"That's the spirit," said Mrs. Schraalenburgh. Next she called on Zoe.

Zoe went to the front of the room and began reading. Cricket was surprised to hear her name in the report. Zoe read, "I picked this book because it was given to me by my friend Cricket Kaufman. At first I thought I wouldn't like it because it was all in letters. But before I knew it, I was right in the middle of the story of Leigh Botts and his problems . . ."

IMPERFECT

Cricket could hardly believe that Zoe considered her to be her friend. Just because she gave her that book it didn't make them friends. That hadn't been her idea. Her mother had insisted that she bring a gift when she went to Zoe's party. And now Zoe had gotten an A writing about it when Cricket had only got a B−. It just didn't seem fair.

Zoe finished reading her report. "How many people want to read that book, now that they have heard about it?" asked Mrs. Schraalenburgh.

Every hand in the class except Cricket's went up.

"Now you know why Zoe got an A on her report. She has done an excellent job of sharing her pleasure with all of us. I notice that Cricket didn't raise her hand. But she doesn't have to read the book. She already did," said the teacher, smiling at Cricket. "And when she gave a copy of it to Zoe as a present, she was sharing her pleasure of the book in still another way."

Cricket could have said that when she bought the book for Zoe, she hadn't even read it yet. But she didn't. She liked what Mrs. Schraalenburgh said about her sharing her pleasure of the book by giving it as a present. It almost made up for the bad mark she got.

P E R F E C T

Mrs. Schraalenburgh wrote Beverly Cleary's name on the chalkboard so that everyone could copy it and said, "Now when you go to the library, you'll know who the author is." Cricket blushed to see the correct spelling on the board. It had really been foolish on her part to write a book report when she didn't have the book right in front of her to copy the author's name. She wouldn't make that mistake again.

A few other students read their book reports too. Cricket noticed that none of them had made covers for their reports. It had been silly of her to waste her time making a fancy cover if Mrs. Schraalenburgh didn't give her extra credit for it.

"There isn't time to read any more reports," said Mrs. Schraalenburgh after a while. "This was just to get us started. Next month, we will have oral book reports and everyone will have a turn. So start looking for a good book to read. Don't wait until the last minute."

The bell rang for dismissal. Zoe edged over to Cricket. "Thanks again for the book," she said.

Cricket nodded her head. She was relieved that Zoe didn't ask her what grade she had gotten on her report. If the situation had been reversed and Cricket had received an A and Zoe had not read her report aloud, Cricket knew she would have been dying to ask.

"I'll bet we have the same taste in books," said Zoe. "Maybe we could go to the library together after school sometime. You could show me the books you've read and I could show you the ones I've read."

Cricket found herself smiling at Zoe. It sounded as if it might be fun. There had never been another girl in school who liked to read as much as she did. Maybe Zoe was right. Maybe she would be a friend to her.

"Okay," she agreed. And suddenly, it didn't matter so much what grade she had gotten on her report. Next time she would get an A. And if Zoe got one too, it wouldn't be so terrible. After all, they were the two smartest girls in Mrs. Schraalenburgh's class.

THINKING ABOUT IT

1 You are in Mrs. Schraalenburgh's class with Cricket, Zoe, and the others. How do you like being there? Why?

2 The author gives her readers some clues that Cricket may not do as well on her book report as she thinks she will. What are some of those clues?

3 Cricket and Zoe are assigned to do a joint project for the science fair. How will they like working together? Will there be any problems? Describe their experience.

Another Book by Johanna Hurwitz

Shy Aldo Sossi is having a terrible time making friends at his new school. His attempts are not made any easier by the disaster that gives him his nickname. Find out how Aldo copes in *Aldo Applesauce*.

CHEATING

BY SUSAN SHREVE

I CHEATED on a unit test in math class this morning during second period with Mr. Burke. Afterward, I was too sick to eat lunch just thinking about it.

I came straight home from school, went to my room, and lay on the floor trying to decide whether it would be better to run away from home now or after supper. Mostly I wished I was dead.

IT WASN'T even an accident that I cheated.

Yesterday Mr. Burke announced there'd be a unit test and anyone who didn't pass would have to come to school on Saturday, most particularly me, since I didn't pass the last unit test. He said that right out in front of everyone as usual. You can imagine how much I like Mr. Burke.

B·27

But I did plan to study just to prove to him that I'm plenty smart—which I am mostly—except in math, which I'd be okay in if I'd memorize my times tables. Anyway, I got my desk ready to study on since it was stacked with about two million things. Just when I was ready to work, Nicho came into my room with our new rabbit and it jumped on my desk and knocked the flashcards all over the floor.

I yelled for my mother to come and help me pick them up, but Carlotta was crying as usual and Mother said I was old enough to help myself and a bunch of other stuff like that which mothers like to say. My mother's one of those people who tells you everything you've done wrong for thirty years like you do it every day. It drives me crazy.

Anyway, Nicho and I took the rabbit outside but then Philip came to my room and also Marty from next door and before long it was dinner. After dinner my father said I could watch a special on television if I'd done all my homework.

Of course I said I had.

That was the beginning. I felt terrible telling my father a lie about the homework so I couldn't even enjoy the special. I guessed he knew I was lying and was so disappointed he couldn't talk about it.

Not much is important in our family. Marty's mother wants him to look okay all the time and my friend Nathan has to do well in school and Andy has so many rules he must go crazy just trying to remember them. My parents don't bother making up a lot of rules. But we do have to tell the truth—even if it's bad, which it usually is. You can imagine how I didn't really enjoy the special.

It was nine o'clock when I got up to my room and that was too late to study for the unit test so I lay in my bed with the light off and decided what I would do the next day when I was in Mr. B.'s math class not knowing the 8- and 9-times tables.

So, you see, the cheating was planned after all.

But at night, thinking about Mr. B.—who could scare just about anybody I know, even my father—it seemed perfectly sensible to cheat. It didn't even seem bad when I thought of my parents' big thing about telling the truth.

I'd go into class jolly as usual, acting like things were going just great, and no one, not even Mr. B., would suspect the truth. I'd sit down next to Stanley Plummer—he is so smart in math it makes you sick—and from time to time, I'd glance over at his paper to copy the answers. It would be a cinch. In fact, every test before, I had to try hard not to see his answers because our desks are practically on top of each other.

And that's exactly what I did this morning. It was a cinch. Everything was okay except that my stomach was upside down and I wanted to die.

THE FACT IS, I couldn't believe what I'd done in cold blood. I began to wonder about myself— really wonder—things like whether I would steal from stores or hurt someone on purpose or do some other terrible thing I couldn't even imagine. I began to wonder whether I was plain bad to the core.

I've never been a wonderful kid that everybody in the world loves and thinks is swell, like Nicho. I have a bad temper and I like to have my own way and I argue a lot. Sometimes I can be mean. But most of the time I've thought of myself as a pretty decent kid. Mostly I work hard, I stick up for little kids, and I tell the truth. Mostly I like myself fine—except I wish I were better at basketball.

Now all of a sudden I've turned into this criminal. It's hard to believe I'm just a boy. And all because of one stupid math test.

Lying on the floor of my room, I begin to think that probably I've been bad all along. It just took this math test to clinch it. I'll probably never tell the truth again.

I tell my mother I'm sick when she calls me to come down for dinner. She doesn't believe me, but puts me to bed anyhow. I lie there in the early winter darkness wondering what terrible thing I'll be doing next when my father comes in and sits down on my bed.

"What's the matter?" he asks.

"I've got a stomachache," I say. Luckily, it's too dark to see his face.

"Is that all?"

"Yeah."

"Mommy says you've been in your room since school."

"I was sick there too," I say.

"She thinks something happened today and you're upset."

That's the thing that really drives me crazy about my mother. She knows things sitting inside my head same as if I was turned inside out.

"Well," my father says. I can tell he doesn't believe me.

"My stomach *is* feeling sort of upset." I hedge.

"Okay," he says and he pats my leg and gets up.

Just as he shuts the door to my room I call out to him in a voice I don't even recognize as my own that I'm going to have to run away.

"How come?" he calls back not surprised or anything.

So I tell him I cheated on this math test. To tell the truth, I'm pretty much surprised at myself. I didn't plan to tell him anything.

He doesn't say anything at first and that just about kills me. I'd be fine if he'd spank me or something. To say nothing can drive a person crazy.

And then he says I'll have to call Mr. Burke.
It's not what *I* had in mind.

"Now?" I ask surprised.

"Now," he says. He turns on the light and pulls off my covers.

"I'm not going to," I say.

But I do it. I call Mr. Burke, probably waking him up, and I tell him exactly what happened, even that I decided to cheat the night before the test. He says I'll come in Saturday to take another test, which is okay with me, and I thank him a whole lot for being understanding and all. He's not friendly but he's not absolutely mean either.

"Today I thought I was turning into a criminal," I tell my father when he turns out my light.

Sometimes my father kisses me good night and sometimes he doesn't. I never know. But tonight he does.

WHAT I KNOW ABOUT "CHEATING"

BY SUSAN SHREVE

Susan Shreve

I cheated on a fifth grade math test. The day before the crime, Ms. Gosnell, our teacher, said that I was the worst math student she had seen in all of her years of teaching (which must have been about a thousand).

I decided how I would get an *A* on the math test the next day. I studied hard and asked my father for help, but he was not much better at math than I was. So I went to bed unprepared.

Just before I fell asleep for my first nightmare of the evening, I decided I would sit next to Douglas Ball and copy off his paper. (I should mention that Douglas got *A*'s in everything.) Douglas was usually lost in his own world of astrology or archeology or mathematics games, so I doubted he would notice what I was doing.

In the morning, I woke up with a terrible stomachache.

I couldn't eat breakfast. I felt weak in my knees and dizzy on the walk to school. My hands were perspiring when the test began, but it was a cinch to see Douglas's paper from where I was sitting.

The next thing I remember, I was in the nurse's office. She said I probably had the stomach flu. I was pale, my face and hands were cold, and my knees were shaking. When my mother arrived, my voice was too thin to talk.

She took me home, put me to bed with a cup of hot tea, and sat on the end of my bed patting my legs. "Don't be nice to me," I said finally. "You should call the police or send for the vice squad."

And then I told her what I had done. She told me that she was proud of me for telling the truth, and certainly my being sick as a dog was sufficient punishment.

But she had a different punishment in mind. Two of them. She found Mrs. Gosnell's telephone number in the book and she knew Douglas's number because he lived next door. Mrs. Gosnell made me repeat what I said to her twice because my voice was so weak.

"Cheated!" she shouted in a voice that could be heard in downtown Washington, D.C. She had me do extra homework and stay in for recess and gym to retake the test.

Douglas was looking at the stars when I called, he told me. "I cheated off your paper in math today," I said so quickly all of the words ran together.

"I know," he said. "I saw."

And that was the last time it crossed my mind to cheat, but I certainly never forgot what happened. Most of my ideas come from my own childhood or that of one of my children or friends. But in every case, I write about situations that I understand as completely as if they had just happened to me.

THINKING ABOUT IT

1 As you began reading, what did you hope would happen in the story?

2 Was the boy's punishment a good one? What in the story shows whether the punishment was a good one or not?

3 Here's a real problem. You have a test coming up. You're worried that you might fail. What will you do?

Another Book by Susan Shreve

One of the worst things that could happen to anyone happens to Joshua—he has to repeat third grade. Does he run away to Siberia? Does he have a temper tantrum? Find out what Joshua's repeated year is like in *The Flunking of Joshua T. Bates.*

Do you remember
learning to read?
That book full of squiggles
like ants escaped,
the teacher's big thumb
on the page,
your heart beating inside
afraid that all you'd ever see
was ants—

Then a word popped out,
"See," and another, "Cat,"
and my finger on teacher's,
we read, "I see cat."
I ran around the room
so happy I saw words
instead of ants.

ANN TURNER

"The Disaster"
by Louis Sachar
from
There's a Boy in the Girls' Bathroom

Jeff Fishkin was hopelessly lost. He clutched his hall pass as he looked down the long empty corridor. The school seemed so big to him.

He was on his way to see the new counselor. She was supposed to help him "adjust to his new environment." Now he not only didn't know how to get to her office, he had no idea how to get back to Mrs. Ebbel's class either.

The floor was slippery. It had started raining during recess and the kids had tracked water and mud inside with them.

A teacher carrying a stack of papers stepped out of a door and Jeff hurried up to her. "Can you tell me where the counselor's office is, please?" he asked. His voice trembled.

The teacher first checked to make sure he had a hall pass. Then she said: "The counselor's office . . . let's see. Go down this hall to the end, turn right, and it's the third door on your left."

"Thank you very much," said Jeff. He started to go.

"No, wait," said the teacher. "That's not right, she's in the new office in the other wing. Turn around and go back the way you just came, then turn left at the end of the hall and it's the second door on your right."

"Thank you," Jeff said again.

He walked to the end of the hall, turned right, counted to the second door on his left, and pushed it open.

A girl with red hair and a freckled face was washing her hands at the sink. When she saw Jeff, her mouth dropped open. "What are you doing in here?" she asked.

"Huh?" Jeff uttered.

"Get out of here!" she yelled. "This is the girls' bathroom!"

Jeff froze. He covered his face with his hands, then dashed out the door.

"THERE'S A BOY IN THE GIRLS' BATHROOM!" the girl screamed after him.

He raced down the hall. Suddenly his feet slipped out from under him. He waved his arms wildly as he tried to keep his balance, then flopped down on the floor.

"Oh no, no, no, oh no, no, no," he groaned. "What have I done? Oh, why didn't I just read the sign on the door? This is the worst day of my whole life!"

Suddenly he realized he was no longer holding the hall pass. He stood up and frantically looked around. "Don't tell me I dropped it in the girls' bathroom."

He heard someone coming and hurried off in the opposite direction. He rounded the corner, then spotted what looked like some kind of storage room. It was cluttered with boxes.

He ducked inside and closed the door behind him.

"Hello," said a voice.

He spun around.

A woman stepped down off a yellow ladder. "You must be Jeff," she said. "I'm Carla Davis." She smiled and held out her hand. "I'm so glad you've come. I was afraid you might get lost."

Jeff sat at the round table. The counselor sat across from him.

"So how do you like Red Hill School?" she asked.

He stared straight ahead. *There's a boy in the girls' bathroom* echoed inside his head.

"I imagine it must seem a little scary," said the counselor.

He didn't answer.

"I think it's scary," she said. "It seems so big! Anytime I try to go anywhere, I get lost."

He smiled weakly.

"It's hard for me because I'm new here," she explained. "Today is only my second day of school. I don't know anybody. Nobody knows me. The other teachers all look at me strangely. It's hard for me to make friends with them. They already have their own friends."

"I know what you mean," Jeff said.

"Maybe you can help me," said the counselor.

"Me?" said Jeff. "How can *I* help *you?* I'm the one who needs help!"

"Well, maybe we can help each other. What do you think about that?"

"How?"

"We're the two new kids at school," she said. "We can share our experiences and learn from each other."

Jeff smiled. "Okay, Miss Davis," he said.

"Jeff," she said, "if we're going to be friends, I want you to call me Carla, not Miss Davis."

He laughed.

"Do you think Carla is a funny name?"

"Oh, no! I just never called a teacher by her first name, that's all."

"But we're friends. Friends don't call each other Miss Davis and Mr. Fishkin, do they?"

Jeff laughed again. "No," he said, then he frowned. "The kids in my class call me Fishface."

"Have you made any friends?" asked Carla.

"I sort of made one friend," said Jeff, "but I don't like him."

"How can he be your friend if you don't like him?"

"Nobody likes him. At first I felt sorry for him because nobody wanted to sit next to him. Mrs. Ebbel said it out loud right in front of the whole class. 'Nobody likes sitting there,' she said. It was like he wasn't even there. It's bad enough when a kid says something like that, but a teacher."

"It must have hurt his feelings," said Carla.

"No. He just smiled."

"He may have been smiling on the outside, but do you think he really was smiling on the inside?"

"I don't know. I guess not. I guess that's why I tried to be friends with him. I told him I liked sitting next to him. But then he said, 'Give me a dollar or I'll spit on you.' "

"What did you do?"

"I gave him a dollar. I didn't want him to spit on me. But then, later, he said, 'I'll give you a dollar to be my friend.' So I took it. It was my dollar! So does that mean I have to be his friend, even though I just broke even?"

"What do you think friendship is?" Carla asked him.

"I don't know. I mean I know what it is, but I can't explain it."

"Is it something you can buy and sell? Can you go to the store and get a quart of milk, a dozen eggs, and a friend?"

Jeff laughed. "No. So does that mean I don't have to be friends with him?"

"I won't tell you what to do," said Carla. "All I can do is help you think for yourself."

"I don't even know if Bradley wants to be my friend," said Jeff. "Today, at recess, we hung around together but we didn't do anything. He acted like I wasn't there. Then, when it started to rain, he ran around trying to push little kids into the mud."

"Could you share your feelings with him?" asked Carla. "That's the real way to build a friendship: by talking, and by being honest and by sharing your feelings. Like the way we're talking and being honest with each other now. That's why we're friends."

"But Bradley's different than you and me," said Jeff.

"I think you'll find that if you're nice to Bradley, he'll be nice to you. If you are honest and friendly with him, he'll be honest and friendly with you. It's just like with the dollar. You always break even."

Jeff smiled. "Are you going to see Bradley too?" he asked.

"Yes, later today."

"Do you think you'll be able to help him?"

"I don't know."

"I hope so. I think he needs help even more than me. You won't tell him anything I said, will you?"

"No, that's one of my most important rules. I never repeat anything anyone tells me here, around the round table."

"Never?"

She shook her head.

"What about to other teachers?"

She shook it again.

"What about to the principal?"

"Nope."

"Okay," said Jeff. He took a breath. "Here goes." He grimaced. "On the way here, I got a little lost, and, um, accidentally went into the girls' bathroom!" He covered his face with his hands.

Mrs. Ebbel was teaching geography. Everybody in the class had a map of the United States on his or her desk.

Bradley's map was different from all the others. California was above Wisconsin. Florida stuck out of Texas. He picked up his pair of scissors and carefully cut out Tennessee. He was a good cutter. The edge of his scissors never left the black line.

He wondered what was happening to Jeff. He knew he was at the counselor's office. He imagined she was doing all kinds of horrible things to him. He had tried to tell Jeff at recess not to go see her.

He taped Tennessee to Washington. He was a very messy taper. His piece of tape twisted and stuck to itself.

He looked up as Jeff entered the room and watched him hang the hall pass on the hook

behind Mrs. Ebbel's desk. Then he looked away as Jeff headed for the seat next to him.

When the bell rang for lunch, he shoved his map into his desk and pulled out his paper sack. Because of the rain, everyone had to eat inside, in the auditorium. He and Jeff walked there together—sort of. *He's walking next to me,* Bradley thought, *but I'm not walking next to him.*

The auditorium was hot, steamy, and noisy. Long tables with benches had been set up across the room.

"Where do you want to sit?" asked Jeff.

Bradley ignored him. He stood on his tiptoes and looked around the room as if he was trying to locate his real friends.

Jeff walked away and sat at one of the tables.

Bradley walked behind where Jeff was sitting. "Hmm, I think I'll sit here," he said aloud, as if he didn't know Jeff was there. He stepped over the bench and sat down next to him.

"Hi," said Jeff.

Bradley faced him for the first time. "Oh, it's you," he said.

They ate their lunches.

"What are you eating?" asked Jeff.

"Peanubudder sandige," said Bradley. As he spoke, bits of peanut butter and bread flew from his mouth. "Wha' bou' you?"

"Tuna fish," said Jeff.

Bradley swallowed his food and said, "I hate tuna fish."

"My mother makes it good," said Jeff. "She
chops apples in it."

"I hate apples," said Bradley. He sucked the
last drop of milk through his straw, then
continued to suck, making a gurgling noise.

Sitting two tables away from Jeff and Bradley
were three girls; Melinda Birch, Lori Westin, and
Colleen Verigold. They were talking and laughing
about something funny that had happened to
Colleen that morning.

Colleen, who had red hair and a freckled face,
covered her mouth with her hand. "There he is!"
she whispered. "It's him!"

"Where?" asked Lori.

"Don't look at him!" said Colleen. "He's right
there, sitting next to Bradley Chalkers."

"Bradley Chalkers," said Lori. "I think I'm going to throw up!"

"Don't look," whispered Colleen.

Bradley stopped sucking on his straw. "What'd the counselor do to you?" he asked.

Jeff shrugged. "Nothing."

"Did she yell a lot? Was she mean and ugly?"

"No. She was nice. I think you'll like her."

"*Me?*" asked Bradley. "I'm not going to see her. I didn't do anything wrong."

"She's good at helping you solve your problems," said Jeff.

"I don't have any problems," said Bradley. He bit ferociously into a red delicious apple.

"I thought you said you hated apples," said Jeff.

Bradley shoved the apple back inside the paper

sack. "That wasn't an apple," he said. "It was a banana."

Jeff's face suddenly changed color, first white, then bright red.

"Ooh, I think he sees you," said Melinda.

Lori laughed.

Colleen blushed.

"C'mon," said Lori. "Let's go talk to him." She stood up. Lori Westin was a short, skinny girl with long straight black hair.

Melinda got up from the table too. She was nearly twice the size of Lori. She had short brown hair.

"No, don't go!" pleaded Colleen.

"What's the matter?" asked Bradley.

"Uh, nothing," said Jeff. "So, did I miss anything in class?"

"No. Mrs. Ebbel gave everybody a map."

"I got one."

"Don't lose it," said Bradley. "Mrs. Ebbel wants them back."

Two girls were giggling behind them.

Jeff and Bradley turned around.

"Colleen thinks you're cute," said Lori.

Jeff blushed. "Who?" he asked.

The girls laughed.

"What's your name?" asked Melinda.

Jeff blushed again.

"*Colleen* wants to know," said Lori, then she and Melinda laughed again.

"He doesn't have a name!" said Bradley, coming to Jeff's rescue. He hated Lori. She had the biggest mouth in the whole school. She was always laughing too. He could hear her laugh from one end of the school to the other.

"E-uuu, Bradley Chalkers!" said Lori, holding her nose.

"Lori Loudmouth!" said Bradley.

"We're not talking to you, Bradley," said Melinda.

"Get out of here or I'll punch your face in," he replied.

"You wouldn't hit a girl," said Melinda.

"That's what you think." He shook his fist.

Melinda and Lori backed away. "We only wanted to know his name," said Melinda.

"And what he was doing in the girls' bathroom!" screeched Lori.

The two girls laughed and ran back to Colleen. Bradley slowly turned and looked at Jeff, amazed. Jeff sat with his head on the table and his arms over his head.

"You went into the girls' bathroom?" Bradley asked.

"So what?" said Jeff from under his elbow. "Carla says—"

"Me too!" declared Bradley. "I go all the time! I like to make them scream!"

He smiled at Jeff.

Bradley Chalkers! What are you doing out of class?"

It was a teacher. Bradley didn't know her, but it seemed as though every teacher in the school knew him. "I got a hall pass!" he told her.

"Let me see it."

He showed it to her. "Mrs. Ebbel gave it to me. Go ask her if you don't believe me."

"Where are you going?"

"Library," he said. "To get a book."

"Okay, but make sure you go straight to the library. No detours, Bradley."

He had lied. He wasn't even allowed to check books out of the library.

The door to the counselor's office was open, so he walked right in. "I'm here," he announced. "Whadda ya want?"

Carla smiled warmly at him. "Hello, Bradley," she said. "I'm Carla Davis. It's a pleasure to see you today." She held out her hand. "I've been looking forward to meeting you."

He was amazed by how young and pretty she was. He had been expecting an ugly old hag.

She had sky-blue eyes and soft blond hair. She wore a white shirt covered with different-colored squiggly lines, like some kid had scribbled on it. But as he stared at the shirt he realized that it was made to look that way, on purpose.

"Aren't you going to shake my hand?" she asked.

"No, you're too ugly." He walked past her and sat down at the round table.

She sat across from him. "I appreciate your coming to see me," she said.

"I had to come. Mrs. Ebbel made me."

"For whatever reason, I'm glad you came."

"I meant to go to the library," he explained. "I came here by accident."

"Oh, I don't believe in accidents," said Carla.

"You don't believe in accidents?" That was the craziest thing he'd ever heard.

She shook her head.

"What about when you spill your milk?"

"Do you like milk?" asked Carla.

"No, I hate it!"

"So maybe you spill it on purpose," she said. "You just think it's an accident." She smiled.

He stared angrily down at the table. He felt like he'd been tricked. "I don't drink milk," he said. "I drink coffee."

He glanced around the room. It was full of all kinds of interesting-looking objects. "This place is a mess," he said.

"I know," Carla admitted. "I like messy rooms. Clean rooms are boring and depressing. They remind me of hospitals."

"Don't you get in trouble?"

"Why should I?"

He didn't know the answer to that. But he knew that if it were his room and it was this messy, he'd get in trouble. "I didn't do anything wrong!" he declared.

"Nobody said you did."

"Well, then how come I have to be here?"

"I was hoping you'd like it here," said Carla. "I was hoping we could be friends. Do you think we can?"

"No."

"Why not?"

"Because I don't like you."

"I like you," said Carla. "I can like you, can't I? You don't have to like me."

He squirmed in his seat.

"I was also hoping you'd be able to teach me things," said Carla.

"You're the teacher, not me."

"So? That doesn't matter. A teacher can often learn a lot more from a student than a student can learn from a teacher."

"I've taught Mrs. Ebbel a lot," Bradley agreed. "Today I taught her geography."

"What do you want to teach me?" Carla asked.

"What do you want to know?"

"You tell me," said Carla. "What's the most important thing you can teach me?"

Bradley tried to think of something he knew. "The elephant's the biggest animal in the world," he said. "But it's afraid of mice."

"I wonder why that is," said Carla.

"Because," said Bradley, "if a mouse ran up an elephant's trunk, it would get stuck and then the elephant wouldn't be able to breathe and so it would die. That's how most elephants die."

"I see," said Carla. "Thank you for sharing that with me. You're a very good teacher."

He suddenly felt like he'd been tricked again. He didn't want to share anything with her. He hated her.

"What else do you want to teach me?" she asked.

"Nothing," he said coldly. "You're not supposed to talk in school."

"Why not?"

"It's a rule. Like no sticking gum in the water fountains."

"Well, in this room there are no rules," said Carla. "In here, everyone thinks for himself. No one tells you what to do."

"You mean I can stick gum in the water fountain?"

"You could, except I don't have a water fountain."

"Can I break something?" he asked.

"Certainly."

He looked around for something to break, then caught himself in time. It was another trick. He'd break something and then get in trouble, and nobody would believe him when he said that she had said there were no rules. "I'm not in the mood," he said.

"All right, but if you are ever in the mood, there are a lot of things you can break—things I like very much and things that other children use."

"I will!" he assured her. "I know karate." He raised his hand sideways over the table. "I can break this table in half with my bare hand."

"I'd hate to see you hurt your hand."

"Nothing ever hurts me," he told her. "I've broken every table in my house," he declared. "The chairs, too. Call my mother if you don't believe me."

"I believe you," said Carla. "Why shouldn't I?"

"You should."

She did too. For the rest of the meeting, no matter what he told her, she believed him.

When he told her that his parents only fed him dog food, she asked him how it tasted.

"Delicious!" he said. "Meaty and sweet."

"I've always wanted to try it," said Carla.

When he told her that the President had called him on the phone last night, she asked what they talked about.

"Hats," he answered right away.

"Hats? What did you say about hats?"

"I asked him why he didn't wear a hat like Abraham Lincoln."

"And what did he say?"

Bradley thought a moment. "I can't tell you. It's top secret."

Near the end of the session, Carla gave him a piece of construction paper and asked him if he wanted to draw a picture. He chose a black crayon from the big box of crayons and stayed with it the whole time. He scribbled wildly all over the paper.

Carla leaned over to look at it. "That's very nice," she said.

"It's a picture of nighttime," he told her.

"Oh. I thought it was a picture of the floor of a barbershop, after someone with black curly hair got his hair cut."

"That's what it is!" Bradley declared. "That's what I meant."

"It's very good," said Carla. "May I have it?"

"What for?"

"I'd like to hang it up on my wall."

He looked at her in amazement. "You mean here?"

"Yes."

"No, it's mine."

"I was hoping you'd share it with me," said Carla.

"It costs a dollar."

"It's worth it," said Carla. "But I only want it if you're willing to share it."

"No," he said.

"Okay, but if you ever change your mind, I'll still want it."

"You can make me give it to you," he suggested.

"No, I can't."

"Sure you can. Teachers make kids do things all the time."

Carla shook her head.

It was time for him to return to class.

"I've enjoyed your visit very much," said Carla. "Thank you for sharing so much with me." She held out her hand.

He backed away from it as if it were some kind of poisonous snake. Then he turned and hurried out into the hall.

When he got to Mrs. Ebbel's class, he crumpled his picture into a ball and dropped it in the wastepaper basket next to her desk.

Thinking About It

Which parts of the story remind you of something that has happened to you or someone you know? Did any of the characters seem like people you've met? Who?

Is Mrs. Ebbel a very understanding person? Is Carla? Why do you say *yes* or why do you say *no?*

Jeff, Bradley, and Carla are on a talk show. They are supposed to talk about "How to Solve Problems." What will you ask them? What will they say?

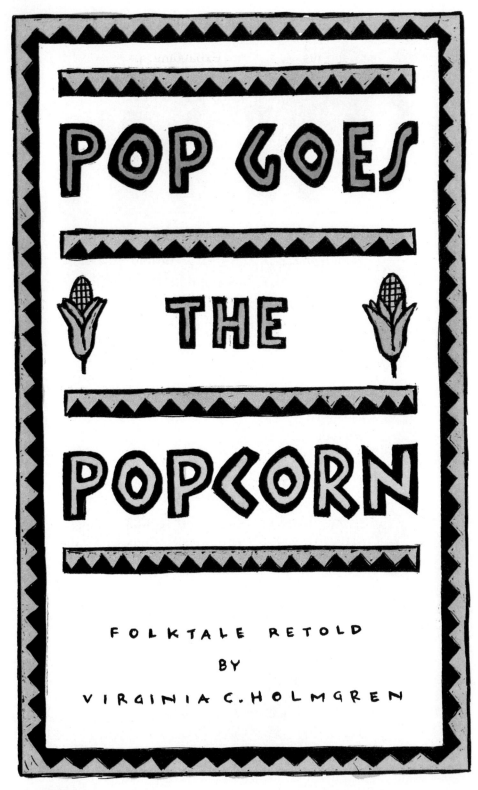

POP GOES THE POPCORN

FOLKTALE RETOLD

BY

VIRGINIA C. HOLMGREN

hico and his grandfather were sitting in the warm Mexican sun sharing a bowl of popcorn.

"Grandfather," Chico said, "why does popcorn pop but corn on the cob doesn't?"

Grandfather chuckled. "That, my boy, used to be a question answered with only one word—magic. Now science gives us two words— hardness and moisture. If there is plenty of inner moisture, it turns to steam as it's heated. The steam keeps expanding, pushing against the kernel's outer shell. If the shell is thin, the steam seeps through, bit by bit. If the shell is hard, it gives way all at once in one grand explosion—pop!"

"Oh," Chico said, frowning. He'd been hoping for one of Grandfather's old-time tales of good spirits, bad spirits, and all kinds of wonders.

Suddenly his frown turned to a grin. "But what about the *magic?*" he asked, sure that a tale would follow. And so it did.

ong, long ago, when the world was still in its
infancy, no corn of any kind grew anywhere in the
world. Here in Mexico, a summer came with no rain,
and the hot sun beat down day after day until almost
every plant dried up and died.

"We must pray to the Rain Spirit!" everyone said.
But how could they pray when they had no flowers to
offer as gifts to win the Rain Spirit's favor? In the
past, they had always woven flowers into wreaths and
garlands to place on the Rain Spirit's sacred stone.
Now they had no choice, and so they prayed with
empty hands. Nothing happened. No rain came—not
a drop.

Suddenly one man could contain his anger no longer.
Shaking his fist at the sky and shouting curses, he
cried, "Hear me, you up there! Hear me!"

The Rain Spirit heard. Anger blacker than any
storm cloud enveloped the Rain Spirit, and he shook
his own fist in reply. He sent icy winds and pelting
rain to punish the people. The raindrops turned to ice
as they fell, pounding down on those gathered at the
altar stone and on everything around it, bruising
tender faces and dry leaves and petals, snapping off
dry twigs, covering everything with pellets of ice.

Wailing, weeping, and moaning, the people begged
forgiveness. For the first time, the Rain Spirit looked
down and saw the damage he had done. How barren
the land was! The people truly had no flowers to offer
him and little food. To make amends for his anger, he

clapped his hands once, twice, and then a third time
and ordered the ice to turn into soft white fluffs as
dainty as any flower.

"Eat!" he commanded. "I give you flowers and food
in one."

Scarcely believing what they heard, the people
slowly began to reach for the pretty fluffs, examining
them with curiosity. A small boy was the first one to
try a taste. Soon he was shoving a whole handful into
his mouth, crying, "Ai-ee! Good! Good!"

Before long, almost everyone else was munching
too, forgetting that the Rain Spirit had said that these
were *flowers* and food. But one grandmother
remembered. Taking out a needle and thread, she
began stringing white fluffs together in a flowerlike
wreath to lay on the altar.

Now the Rain Spirit was really pleased. He told them where to find plants with seeds that would turn into these fluffs and how to prepare this dry-season food. And that is how popcorn came to Mexico's ancient ones.

In time, the people would have sweet corn and field corn too, but popcorn came first, and it was honored each year on a special day. That day, which came just as the summer dry season began (at the end of May or the beginning of June by today's calendar) was set aside as Thanks-for-Popcorn Day. Specially selected men and maidens donned popcorn wreaths and garlands and danced while pipers played a hop-pop tune on little clay flutes and everyone watched and cheered. Everyone ate popcorn, and everyone made popcorn flower wreaths for the Rain Spirit in thanks for his rain and for this special gift. Thanks-for-Popcorn Day is no longer celebrated, but popcorn will never be forgotten.

 s Grandfather finished his tale, Chico held out the empty bowl. "Let's make more," he said. "One Popcorn Day a year may have been enough for the ancients, but I'm ready to celebrate all year. Aren't you?"

THINKING ABOUT IT

 Chico wonders why popcorn pops. What things in nature do you wonder about?

 Why was popcorn important to the people of Mexico long ago?

 A five-year-old asks you a question, such as "Why is the sky blue?" or "Why do raisins have wrinkles?" What is your answer? Think up a question a young child might ask and provide two answers—one using facts from science and one from your imagination.

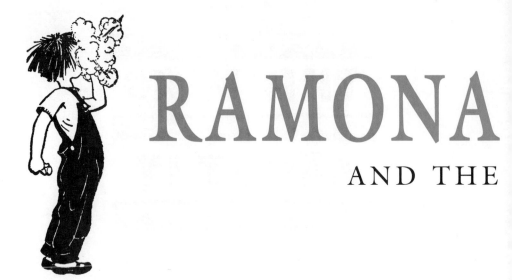

RAMONA

AND THE

MOTHER, I'm home," Beezus called, as she burst into the house one afternoon after school.

Mother appeared, wearing her hat and coat and carrying a shopping list in her hand. She kissed Beezus. "How was school today?" she asked.

"All right. We studied about Christopher Columbus," said Beezus.

"Did you, dear?" said Mother absent-mindedly. "I wonder if you'd mind keeping an eye on Ramona for half an hour or so while I do the marketing. She was up so late last night I let her have a long nap this afternoon, and I wasn't able to go out until she woke up."

"All right, I'll look after her," agreed Beezus.

"I told her she could have two marshmallows," said Mother, as she left the house.

Ramona came out of the kitchen with a marshmallow in each hand. Her nose was covered with white powder. "What's Christopher Colummus?" she asked.

"Christopher Columbus," Beezus corrected. "Come here, Ramona. Let me wipe off your nose."

APPLES *by* BEVERLY CLEARY

"No," said Ramona, backing away. "I just powdered it." Closing her eyes, Ramona pounded one of the marshmallows against her nose. Powdered sugar flew all over her face. "These are my powder puffs," she explained.

Beezus started to tell Ramona not to be silly, she'd get all sticky, but then decided it would be useless. Ramona never minded being sticky. Instead, she said, "Christopher Columbus is the man who discovered America. He was trying to prove that the world is round."

"Is it?" Ramona sounded puzzled. She beat the other marshmallow against her chin.

"Why, Ramona, don't you know the world is round?" Beezus asked.

Ramona shook her head and powdered her forehead with a marshmallow.

"Well, the world is round just like an orange," Beezus told her. "If you could start out and travel in a perfectly straight line you would come right back where you started from."

"I would?" Ramona looked as if she didn't understand this at all. She also looked as if she didn't care much, because she went right on powdering her face with the marshmallows.

Oh, well, thought Beezus, there's no use trying to explain it to her. She went into the bedroom to change from her school clothes into her play clothes. As usual, she found Ramona's doll, Bendix, lying on her bed, and with a feeling of annoyance she tossed it across the room to Ramona's bed. When she had changed her clothes she went into the kitchen, ate some graham crackers and peanut butter, and helped herself to two marshmallows. If Ramona could have two, it was only fair that she should have two also.

After eating the marshmallows and licking the powdered sugar from her fingers, Beezus decided that reading about Big Steve would be the easiest way to keep Ramona from thinking up some mischief to get into while Mother was away. "Come here, Ramona," she said as she went into the living room. "I'll read to you."

There was no answer. Ramona was not there.

That's funny, thought Beezus, and went into the bedroom. The room was empty. I wonder where she can be, said Beezus to herself. She looked in Mother and Father's room. No one was there. "Ramona!" she called. No answer. "Ramona, where are you?" Still no answer.

Beezus was worried. She did not think Ramona had left the house, because she had not heard any doors open and close. Still, with Ramona you never knew. Maybe she was hiding. Beezus

looked under the beds. No Ramona. She looked in
the bedroom closets, the hall closet, the linen closet,
even the broom closet. Still no Ramona. She ran
upstairs to the attic and looked behind the trunks.

Then she ran downstairs to the basement.
"Ramona!" she called anxiously, as she peered
around in the dim light. The basement was an
eerie place with its gray cement walls and the
grotesque white arms of the furnace reaching out
in all directions. Except for a faint sound from the
pilot light everything was silent. Suddenly the
furnace lit itself with such a whoosh that Beezus,

her heart pounding, turned and ran upstairs. Even though she knew it was only the furnace, she could not help being frightened. The house seemed so empty when no one answered her calls.

Uneasily Beezus sat down in the living room to try to think while she listened to the silence. She must not get panicky. Ramona couldn't be far away. And if she didn't turn up soon, she would telephone the police, the way Mother did the time Ramona got lost because she started out to find the pot of gold at the end of the rainbow.

Thinking of the rainbow reminded Beezus of her attempt to explain to Ramona that the world is round like an orange. Ramona hadn't looked as if she understood, but sometimes it was hard to tell about Ramona. Maybe she just understood the part about coming back where she started from. If Ramona set out to walk to the end of the rainbow, she could easily decide to try walking around the world. That was exactly what she must have done.

The idea frightened Beezus. How would she ever find Ramona? And what would Mother say when she came home and found Ramona gone? To think of Ramona walking in a straight line, hoping to go straight around the world and come back where she started from, trying to cross busy streets alone, honked at by trucks, barked at by strange dogs, tired, hungry . . . But I can't just sit here, thought Beezus. I've got to do something. I'll run out and look up and down the street. She can't have gone far.

At that moment Beezus heard a noise. She thought it came from the basement, but she was not certain. Tiptoeing to the cold-air intake in the hall, she bent over and listened. Sure enough, a noise so faint she could scarcely hear it came up through the furnace pipe. So the house wasn't empty after all! Just wait until she got hold of Ramona!

Beezus snapped on the basement light and ran down the steps. "Ramona, come out," she ordered. "I know you're here."

The only answer was a chomping sound from the corner of the basement. Beezus ran around the furnace and there, in the dimly lit corner, sat Ramona, eating an apple.

Beezus was so relieved to see Ramona safe, and at the same time so angry with her for hiding, that she couldn't say anything. She just stood there filled with the exasperated mixed-up feeling that Ramona so often gave her.

"Hello," said Ramona through a bite of apple.

"Ramona Geraldine Quimby!" exclaimed Beezus, when she had found her voice. "What do you think you're doing?"

"Playing hide-and-seek," answered Ramona.

"Well, I'm not!" snapped Beezus. "It takes two to play hide-and-seek."

"You found me," Ramona pointed out.

"Oh . . ." Once again Beezus couldn't find any words. To think she had worried so, when all the time Ramona was sitting in the basement listening to her call. And eating an apple too!

As she stood in front of Ramona, Beezus' eyes began to grow accustomed to the dim light and she realized what Ramona was doing. She stared, horrified at what she saw. As if hiding were not enough! What would Mother say when she came home and found what Ramona had been up to this time?

Ramona was sitting on the floor beside a box of apples. Lying around her on the cement floor were a number of apples—each with one bite out of it. While Beezus stared, Ramona reached into the box, selected an apple, took one big bite out of the reddest part, and tossed the rest of the apple onto the floor. While she noisily chewed that bite, she reached into the apple box again.

"Ramona!" cried Beezus, horrified. "You can't do that."

"I can too," said Ramona through her mouthful.

"Stop it," ordered Beezus. "Stop it this instant! You can't eat one bite and then throw the rest away."

"But the first bite tastes best," explained Ramona reasonably, as she reached into the box again.

Beezus had to admit that Ramona was right. The first bite of an apple always did taste best. Ramona's sharp little teeth were about to sink into another apple when Beezus snatched it from her.

"That's my apple," screamed Ramona.

"It is not!" said Beezus angrily, stamping her foot. "One apple is all you're supposed to have. Just wait till Mother finds out!"

Ramona stopped screaming and watched Beezus. Then, seeing how angry Beezus was, she smiled and offered her an apple. "I want to share the apples," she said sweetly.

"Oh, no, you don't," said Beezus. "And don't try to work that sharing business on me!" That was one of the difficult things about Ramona. When she had done something wrong, she often tried to get out of it by offering to share something. She heard a lot about sharing at nursery school.

Now what am I going to do, Beezus wondered. I promised Mother I would keep an eye on Ramona, and look what she's gone and done. How am I going to explain this to Mother? I'll get scolded too. And all the apples. What can we do with them?

Beezus was sure about one thing. She no longer felt mixed up about Ramona. Ramona was perfectly impossible. She snatched Ramona's hand. "You come upstairs with me and be good until Mother gets back," she ordered, pulling her sister up the basement stairs.

Ramona broke away from her and ran into the living room. She climbed onto a chair, where she sat with her legs sticking straight out in front of her. She folded her hands in her lap and said in a little voice, "Don't bother me. This is my quiet time. I'm supposed to be resting."

Quiet times were something else Ramona had learned about at nursery school. When she didn't

want to do something, she often insisted she was supposed to be having a quiet time. Beezus was about to say that Ramona didn't need a quiet time, because she hadn't been playing hard and Mother had said she had already had a nap, but then she thought better of it. If Ramona wanted to sit in a chair and be quiet, let her. She might stay out of mischief until Mother came home.

Beezus had no sooner sat down to work on her pot holders, planning to keep an eye on Ramona at the same time, when the telephone rang. It must be Aunt Beatrice, she thought, before she answered. Mother and Aunt Beatrice almost always talked to each other about this time of day.

"Hello, darling, how are you?" asked Aunt Beatrice.

"Oh, Aunt Beatrice," cried Beezus, "Ramona has just done something awful, and I was supposed to be looking after her. I don't know what to do." She told about Ramona's hiding in the cellar and biting into half a box of apples.

Aunt Beatrice laughed. "Leave it to Ramona to think up something new," she said. "Do you know what I'd do if I were you?"

"What?" asked Beezus eagerly, already feeling better because she had confided her troubles to her aunt.

"I wouldn't say anything more about it," said Aunt Beatrice. "Lots of times little children are naughty because they want to attract attention. I have an idea that saying nothing about her naughtiness will worry Ramona more than a scolding."

Beezus thought this over and decided her aunt was right. If there was one thing Ramona couldn't stand, it was being ignored. "I'll try it," she said.

"And about the apples," Aunt Beatrice went on. "All I can suggest is that your mother might make applesauce."

This struck Beezus as being funny, and as she and her aunt laughed together over the telephone she felt much better.

"Tell your mother I phoned," said Aunt Beatrice.

"I will," promised Beezus. "And please come over soon."

When Beezus heard her mother drive up, she rushed out to meet her and tell her the story of what Ramona had done. She also told her Aunt Beatrice's suggestion.

"Oh, dear, leave it to Ramona," sighed Mother. "Your aunt is right. We won't say a word about it."

Beezus helped her mother carry the groceries into the house. Ramona came into the kitchen to see if there were any animal crackers among the packages. She waited a few minutes for her sister to tattle on her. Then, when Beezus did not say anything, she announced, "I was bad this afternoon." She sounded pleased with herself.

"Were you?" remarked Mother calmly. "Beezus, I think applesauce would be good for dessert tonight. Will you run down and bring up some apples?"

When Ramona looked disappointed at having failed to arouse any interest, Beezus and her mother exchanged smiles. "I want to help," said Ramona, rather than be left out.

Beezus and Ramona made four trips to the basement to bring up all the bitten apples. Mother said nothing about their appearance, but spent the rest of the afternoon peeling and cooking apples. After she had finished, she filled her two largest mixing bowls, a casserole, and the bowl of her electric mixer with applesauce. It took her quite a while to rearrange the contents of the refrigerator to make room for all the applesauce.

When Beezus saw her father coming home she ran out on the front walk to tell him what had happened. He too, agreed that Aunt Beatrice's suggestion was a good one.

"Daddy!" shrieked Ramona when her father came in.

"How's my girl?" asked Father as he picked Ramona up and kissed her.

"Oh, I was bad today," said Ramona.

"Were you?" said Father as he put her down. "Was there any mail today?"

Ramona looked crestfallen. "I was very bad," she persisted. "I was awful."

Father sat down and picked up the evening paper.

"I hid from Beezus and I bit lots and lots of apples," Ramona went on insistently.

"Mmm," remarked Father from behind the paper. "I see they're going to raise bus fares again."

"Lots and lots of apples," repeated Ramona in a loud voice.

"They raised bus fares last year," Father went on, winking at Beezus from behind the paper. "The public isn't going to stand for this."

Ramona looked puzzled and then disappointed, but she did not say anything.

Father dropped his paper. "Something certainly smells good," he said. "It smells like applesauce. I hope so. There's nothing I like better than a big dish of applesauce for dessert."

Because Mother had been so busy making applesauce, dinner was a little late that night. At the table Ramona was unusually well behaved. She did not interrupt and she did not try to share her carrots, the way she usually did because she did not like carrots.

As Beezus cleared the table and Mother served dessert—which was fig Newtons and, of course, applesauce—Ramona's good behavior continued. Beezus found she was not very hungry for applesauce, but the rest of the family appeared to enjoy it. After Beezus had wiped the dishes for

Mother she sat down to embroider her pot holders. She had decided to give Aunt Beatrice the pot holder with the dancing knife and fork on it instead of the one with the laughing teakettle.

Ramona approached her with *Big Steve the Steam Shovel* in her hand. "Beezus, will you read to me?" she asked.

She thinks I'll say no and then she can make a fuss, thought Beezus. Well, I won't give her a chance. "All right," she said, putting down her pot holder and taking the book, while Ramona climbed into the chair beside her.

"Big Steve was a steam shovel. He was the biggest steam shovel in the whole city," Beezus read. " 'Gr-r-r,' growled Big Steve when he moved the earth to make way for the new highway."

Father dropped his newspaper and looked at his two daughters sitting side by side. "I wonder," he said, "exactly how long this is going to last."

"Just enjoy it while it does," said Mother, who was basting patches on the knees of a pair of Ramona's overalls.

"Gr-r-r," growled Ramona. "Gr-r-r."

Beezus also wondered just how long this would go on. She didn't enjoy growling like a steam shovel and she felt that perhaps Ramona was getting her own way after all. I'm trying to like her like I'm supposed to, anyhow, Beezus thought, and I do like her more than I did this afternoon when I found her in the basement. But what on earth will Mother ever do with all that applesauce?

THINKING
ABOUT IT

1 Who have you known who is like Ramona? Have *you* been someone like Ramona? Are you glad? Are you sorry? Tell about the experience.

2 Beezus has to put up with several annoying things Ramona does. What are they, and how does she cope with them?

3 Beezus convinces you to baby-sit for Ramona Saturday afternoon. What will you do to entertain Ramona? How will you make sure she doesn't get into trouble?

Yani's Monkeys

by Scarlet Cheng

AN EAGER CROWD of parents and children have gathered at the Arthur M. Sackler Gallery in Washington, D.C., to watch Wang Yani from the People's Republic of China demonstrate her remarkable skill in painting. Wang Yani—only fourteen years old—is already recognized in her native country and around the world as a gifted artist. Her paintings have been shown in art galleries and museums throughout China, Asia, and Europe—and recently in three cities in the United States. For the opening of a major exhibition of her works, the Sackler Gallery has invited the young artist to visit the United States.

Before she begins her demonstration, Yani closes her eyes for a moment of meditation. Then, ignoring the curious crowd, she looks

at the large blank sheet of paper before her—four by six feet. In her mind she is composing a picture.

Yani begins her painting by throwing the contents of a small bowl of dark ink across the diagonal of the paper. This becomes the trunk of a gnarled tree. With a brush she paints branches coming from the trunk. Circles made with pink quickly become the petals of plum blossoms.

Upon a horizontal branch she places a red face attached to a fuzzy dark body, finishing it with a curled tail. The audience laughs with delight to recognize that it is a monkey—one of Yani's favorite subjects.

In a brisk twenty minutes she is done. When asked how she feels, she says in her small, whispery voice, "I feel very happy."

Born in Gongcheng, China, in a small city near the river Li and the scenic mountains of Guilin, Wang Yani was lucky to have both talent and parents who encouraged her. Her father, Wang Shiqiang, was a painter who gave up his own career to help hers. "I've learned from Yani too," he says. "I've learned about freedom of expression and about feeling young again."

His daughter began drawing at the age of two

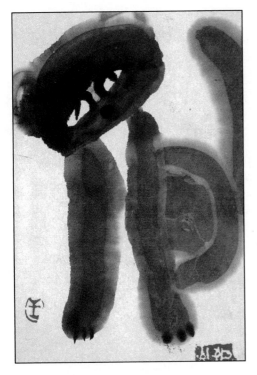

Kitty, 1978–79, age three

Yani likes to paint large and spontaneously, without planning in advance. Her style falls into the Chinese tradition of *xie yi* or "idea painting." Interestingly enough, she likes to listen to Western classical music when she paints. It inspires her and helps her to concentrate. The music of Ludwig van Beethoven is her favorite.

When Yani was three, she became fascinated by the rambunctious monkeys on a visit to the zoo. They made funny faces at her, they shrieked and scurried about, they played happily on their swing. Afterward Yani often begged to go and see them again. One day, when she was six, her father brought home a special gift: a pet monkey she named Lida.

From carefully observing Lida and other real monkeys, Yani began to draw her monkeys more realistically. Before, she had drawn them with seven fingers on each

and a half. When she was old enough to hold a brush, he bought her brushes, inks, and paper. Yani uses brushes made with animal-hair tips and bamboo handles and applies the special watercolor inks to a very absorbent paper. These are basic materials that have been used in Chinese painting for hundreds of years.

Pull Harder, 1980, age five

hand, but when she noticed that they really have five fingers, that's what she started to draw instead. (You can count them too, if you look at one of her pictures!)

Yani painted monkeys often, and she became known for them, first in her province, then eventually throughout China. Though she paints her monkeys with just a few broad strokes of the brush, those strokes capture both the anatomy and the wonderful playfulness of these lively creatures.

In her paintings the monkeys are sometimes by themselves, but usually they are playing with their friends or getting in trouble. With each picture Yani invents a story. Sometimes the monkeys are climbing trees to shake loquats (a Chinese fruit) down to the ground. Sometimes they're dancing with blue and red butterflies or playing tug of war. In one

Let's Go Pick Some Cherries, 1984, age nine

Pretty Riverbanks, 1986, age ten

work she even shows them learning to paint with ink and brush!

Without formal training in art, Yani paints what interests her. Her father has said, "If you ask her to copy something, it's never as vivid as when she draws from her mind. And that's as it should be. After all, she's not a camera!" Sometimes Yani paints people and landscapes, but she prefers her imaginative world of birds and flowers, monkeys and trees.

Like other Chinese children, Yani attends school Monday through Friday, from 6:45 in the morning until 9:30 at night. Since her school is within walking distance, she rushes home during lunch and dinner breaks to paint. "From 11:40 to 12:20, and then from 5:20 to 6:00," she says precisely. On Saturdays she has class from morning until late in the afternoon, with a little time for playing with friends afterward. On Sunday Yani does her homework in the morning, her painting in the afternoon, and then goes back in the evening for two and a half more hours of school.

Although Yani takes many courses—from history to English—she does not take art class. "The art teacher once criticized my work," Yani says simply. "So I never went back."

When there are exhibitions of her work, she travels with her father to attend them. Often she gives demonstrations to crowds, who are amazed to see how fast she works and how animals and other recognizable objects emerge from the slashes and blobs of paint she puts to paper. Though some strokes seem accidental, Yani manages to weave everything into her picture.

Other children especially enjoy her playful, mischievous monkeys, chickens, cats, and other animals. They are also glad to see adults taking her work seriously.

While Yani paints for herself, she likes other people to see and appreciate her work. "When people see my pictures," Yani says, "I want them to know what's on my mind."

What are her plans for the future? "Mmmm, I haven't thought that far ahead." Then she says with a little smile, "I suppose I just want to keep painting."

Thinking About It

1. You are Yani, thinking aloud as you create a painting. What do you say?

2. Can you get to know an artist by looking at that artist's paintings? Try. Look at Yani's paintings and read about Yani—and then explain what you're learning about her.

3. Produce or describe an art work that tells about you.

The Porcupine

Rebecca Jane,
a friend of mine,
went out to pat
a porcupine.

She very shortly
came back in,
disgusted with
the porcupin.

"One never, ever
should," said Jane,
"go out and pat
a porcupain!"

N. M. BODECKER

74th Street

Hey, this little kid gets roller skates.
She puts them on.
She stands up and almost
flops over backwards.
She sticks out a foot like
she's going somewhere and
falls down and
smacks her hand. She
grabs hold of a step to get up and
sticks out the other foot and
slides about six inches and
falls and
skins her knee.

    And then, you know what?

She brushes off the dirt and the
blood and puts some
spit on it and then
sticks out the other foot

    again.

MYRA COHN LIVINGSTON

What If . . .

What if . . .
    You opened a book
    About dinosaurs
And one stumbled out
And another and another
    And more and more pour
Until the whole place
Is bumbling and rumbling
And groaning and moaning
    And snoring and roaring
And dinosauring?

What if . . .
    You tried to push them
    Back inside
But they kept tromping
Off the pages instead?
    Would you close the covers?

ISABEL JOSHLIN GLASER

RIDE THE

by
Harriette
Gillem
Robinet

RED CYCLE

Jerome's got something to say,
Mama, and you gotta listen!"

Jerome felt a warm blush rise up from his
neck as Tilly, his fifteen-year-old sister, spoke for
him. He wished she wouldn't do that. It made him
feel he wasn't real.

Once he had liked the word *special,* special
classes, special bus. Then he decided it meant
"not like other boys."

The trouble was that people were always
helping him. His speech was slow and slurred,
and someone was always finishing what he wanted
to say. When he played baseball, he would kneel
to bat the ball and someone would run the bases
for him. When he tried to roll his wheelchair at
school, one of the kids would insist on pushing it.
Everything happened to him, but he never got a

chance to make things happen himself. Like a chick breaking out of an egg, he wanted to break free.

Sitting at the breakfast table on that sunny spring morning, he felt a little dizzy; his heart beat faster, the room looked fuzzy to him. It was now or never, he thought. Would they laugh at him? It didn't matter, this was something he had to do. He had to make a break, and this was how he was going to do it. There was a dream that haunted him, and he had to do something about that dream. He wished he spoke more clearly, but since he couldn't, he asked very slowly.

"I wann tricycle to rrr-ride!"

"How's Jerome gonna ride, when he can't walk yet, Papa?" Liza asked innocently. Jerome picked up his fork and struck her on the arm; when she screamed, he made a face at her.

"Jerome, you stop that!" Mama said. She looked thin and nervous, her fingers tapped on the table.

Round-faced Liza was only five, but already she could ride Tilly's big two-wheeler. She didn't mean to hurt anyone when she reminded the family that eleven-year-old Jerome, who was in the fifth grade, couldn't even walk.

As a baby, he had walked at nine months. By his first birthday he was running around strong. But when he was two years old, a virus infection had gone to his brain and left damage that affected his whole body. When he got better, he had to learn to support his head, turn over, and crawl all over again. And his legs remained crippled.

Nervous and angry, Mama began clearing the breakfast table even though no one was finished. Papa, Liza, Tilly, and plump little three-year-old Gordon grabbed at toast as Mama whisked plates away.

"That ungrateful boy," Mama grumbled, "never says thank you, but always demandin' somethin'. It's take him here, take him there. Clinics, doctors, physical therapy, speech therapy. Seems that's all I do, take Jerome Johnson somewheres. Now he want a tricycle at eleven years old. Lordy, what's comin' next?"

Papa, a short stocky man with dark brown skin, cleared his throat. "What *they* say, Mary?"

Jerome felt angry tears springing into his eyes. He felt so angry he hit Gordon under the table and Gordon started to cry. Jerome's throat ached from wanting to cry too, but he couldn't blink or someone would notice.

He didn't mind what Mama said, she was always grumbling. Besides, Mama was fussing because she was scared that her big son couldn't ride a tricycle. He knew how his mother felt because he was scared himself. But how would he ever find out if he never tried? No, he wasn't angry with Mama, but Papa wanted to know what *they* had to say.

All his life *they*—all the people in his life that other boys never had to worry about—got to say things about him.

They were the physical therapists who exercised his legs, the speech therapists, the bone doctors, the nerve doctors, the eye doctors, and the social workers who got money for Mama to pay for his braces and his special shoes and his eyeglasses and his wheelchair. *They* were all the people he had to be grateful to. He was tired of being grateful. He hated to say thank you. It got stuck in his throat.

They made all the decisions in his life; but just once he wanted to do something all by himself! This time he didn't care what *they* said. He had thought for a long time, and he had chosen carefully for himself. A teenager with cerebral palsy told him that a two-wheeler was out of the question. It took balance to ride a two-wheeler. But three wheels . . .

Of course he was pleased with the wheelchair. He got around the neighborhood with it, except for curbs. Until he was six, his folks had carried him like a bundle of newspapers.

The wheelchair was all right, but Jerome had a wonderful dream. In it he was speeding fast, with the wind in his face, eyes squinted tight, leaning forward like the leather-jacket guys on motorcycles. That was his dream, and in his dream hundreds of thousands watched as he raced along a track. Cheers and clapping sounded like thunder in the sky. He was reckless and calm and cool, and millions knew his name. And as he stepped off his cycle, he walked with a casual swagger. Jerome Johnson, cycle rider!

All right, he couldn't race a motorcycle, but he had seen a gray-haired man on a three-wheel cycle once, the kind of cycle he wanted. Summer vacation started in a few weeks, and with real wheels he would be able to go everywhere. He didn't care what *they* said. Oh! for a set of wheels!

Mama answered Papa softly.

"John, physical therapist say it be good leg motion, good for his legs. But Dr. Ryan say that left leg real spastic-stiff."

Then in a louder voice aimed at Jerome, she said, "'Sides, that boy's gotta learn to be grateful for what he got!"

"Ha!" Papa jumped at the mention of Dr. Ryan. "Dr. Ryan didn't think he could learn to crawl neither, but he did. I think the boy oughta have a tricycle!"

"Hey now, Papa!" Tilly said triumphantly. "Jerome and me'll be ready to go shopping when you come home." Saturdays Papa worked half-day at the post office.

Mama finished clearing the breakfast table and went to tell the news to Mrs. Mullarkey, the next-door neighbor. Liza, her round face grinning, and little brother Gordon ran out to play. Tilly, tall and thin, dug her hands into her skirt pockets and followed. She sighed. It looked like Jerome was off again. But she knew that no matter what he did, she'd always back him up.

Jerome sat alone in his wheelchair. He wore a green shirt and short brown pants that he hated because his leg braces showed. He was so excited that his eyeglasses steamed up on the inside. He took them off and cleaned them with a tissue. When he put them back on, the room changed from a lazy blur to the sharply outlined kitchen. The round table and chairs showed a hint of white paint on their scrubbed wooden surfaces. Dishes were stacked neatly on clean open shelves across from him.

He had worn eyeglasses since the virus. He thought they made him look smart, like a professor; other people said he looked like an angry owl. These particular glasses were a victory for him. When he broke his last frames, he had demanded thick black rims.

"I won't wear any pale eyeglasses," he had said.

But the eyeglass man said, "We don't have black rims for a child that age . . ."

While the man was talking, Tilly found some in the eyeglass catalogue. It took an extra two weeks for them to come, but at last he got the thick black frames for his big, sparkling black eyes.

He had to admit Tilly sometimes knew how he felt. She was the one who made sure the kids called him his full name. He hated being called Jerry; it sounded like a girl's name or a baby's name to him. With Tilly's help he was called Jerome. He thought Jerome Johnson had a noble sound!

And he liked his extra-strong brown arms and broad shoulders too. His arms had grown strong from supporting him when his legs wouldn't. But he hated his skinny legs and the braces he wore attached to high-top shoes. None of that would matter, though, when he got his three-wheel cycle.

Whirling in his chair, he saw a limp balloon on the kitchen sideboard. It was one Gordon had been playing with. He reached over, grabbed it and tried to pop it with his broad clumsy hands. Straining violently, half-afraid but wanting to hear the loud bang, he grunted, "Brrr-reak balloonnn."

It was too hard. His hands were too stiff to pop the silly old balloon. Something else he couldn't do.

Outside, Gordon overheard Jerome say "break balloon" just as Papa was coming home from work. Breathless, Gordon met his father.

"Papa, Papa," Gordon called. "Jerome's gonna make the moon—he gonna ride his cycle to the moon, Papa?"

Papa smiled wearily and hugged Gordon. He didn't know where that little boy got his wild ideas! Inside, Tilly and Jerome were ready to go shopping, and they were soon on their way.

In the bicycle shop window, Jerome saw what he wanted. The seat was higher than those on small two-wheelers, the wheels were really big, and the color was orange-fire red. It was redder than any fire engine would dare to be.

"Papa, Uh wannn-n tha' un," he called out.

Oh! He could feel the wind whizzing through his soft black kinky hair as he sped along the highways. Highways? Well, along the sidewalk anyway.

Tilly pushed his wheelchair straight up to the big three-wheel cycle while Papa went to get a salesman. There was no price tag on the cycle, and he was afraid to hope. His heart beat faster and he felt breathless for the second time that day. He was so close, this was the cycle he wanted. Would it cost too much?

He was thrilled and happy and afraid too. Maybe Mama was right and he was being foolish. Just then Jerome saw Tilly's foot. He turned his wheelchair quickly and ran over it. He didn't mean to exactly, but he was anxious and getting angry. Papa hadn't come back yet.

Tilly yelled out and looked at him sharply. Why was her brother so mean? Here she was backing him up and he was mean to her again. Why did she ever bother with Jerome? The hurt brought tears to her eyes, but Jerome didn't say he was sorry.

Papa came back and lifted his son onto the seat of the big red cycle. It must be all right; he'll buy it for me, Jerome thought. He gripped the handles and noticed red and white streamers on the plastic handle grips—how they would fly in the wind as he rode! But he felt shaky, up so high on the seat, and as he held on and looked around, Papa noticed.

"Never you mind, son, I'll build up the pedals and make the seat broader," Papa told him. Then to the salesman he said, "We'll take this 'un."

Papa paid at the cash register, and soon Jerome was riding home with his dream cycle tied down in the trunk of the car.

At the house, Mama and Mrs. Mullarkey were standing in the sunshine talking. Jerome was glad Mama hadn't gone to the bicycle shop. She would have made a fuss over the price and would have made him thank Papa, thank the salesman. He didn't thank anybody.

"Lord-a-mighty! What's that?" Mama said, shocked at the big, bright-red, shiny cycle.

"Boy's gonna kill himself on that, Mary!" Mrs. Mullarkey whispered.

Jerome slid out of the car onto the sidewalk. He crawled past Tilly who reached to help him; he crawled past Papa who unfolded his wheelchair for him. He kneeled up straight and, looking at Mama and Mrs. Mullarkey, he said slowly, "Here muhhh cycle. Papa gonna fit it for to rrr-ride!"

Then he lumbered across the grass, up the steps, and into the house. He would show them, maybe, he thought. Everyone watched him in silence.

Suddenly Mama called after him. "Hope yuh told yuh Papa thank you!"

Papa frowned at Mama and said, "Boy don't havta be beholdin' to no one."

Tilly thought, he could've said he was sorry, though, when he ran over my foot.

It took Papa almost a week of evenings after work to finish outfitting the cycle. He attached wooden blocks to the pedals and put leather straps on the blocks to hold his son's shoes. Without the straps Jerome couldn't keep his feet on the pedals.

Since his son kept sliding off the seat, Papa made a new one. From a secondhand chair he got a plastic seat and back, all in one piece. He drilled holes and screwed the new seat onto the cycle, then put a seat belt around it.

On the first of June, Jerome sat on his cycle outdoors for the first time, but he didn't try riding until Papa came home. Everyone was excited. Kids and their mothers from the other row houses on the block gathered on his front doorsteps. For the millionth time Mama told them how much trouble he had been because he wasn't grateful for just being alive.

"Lordy, I never thought my boy'd be livin' today, the way he was. He lay there two weeks, didn't know nobody. All but dead before he come to." Mama was always harping on how sick he had been with the virus.

One mother told Mama he was a brave boy, but Mama shook her head. "Stubborn and foolish," she said.

Neighborhood kids were riding their bicycles in circles and then standing astride them. Liza, a proud grin across her face, rode up and down the block calling people to come see her brother's new cycle.

Jerome thought Mama looked a little proud of him in spite of what she said. She stood on the steps with her thin arms crossed tightly. He was glad people were calling it a cycle and not a tricycle. It was big enough not to look like the tricycles little Gordon's friends rode.

When Papa came home, he pulled his son's handlebars slowly and showed him how to push from his knees to pedal. Jerome leaned forward panting, his tongue showing, but his legs wouldn't move. His legs wouldn't move!

He wiped at the silver stream of drool that soaked his shirt. He only drooled now when he was nervous, and with all those people watching, he was nervous. His legs trembled and he felt cold with his sweat and saliva drying in the breeze.

After a while the neighbors and kids grew tired of watching him and they agreed it would be a long time before he learned to ride, if ever. As they began drifting away, he felt disappointment drape over him like a dead man's shirt. He didn't really expect to ride the first day, but somehow he had hoped . . .

The kids went their ways, calling noisily to each other and racing off on bicycles, but Papa and Tilly stayed, giving him pushes.

"Papa, yook, eh catch," Jerome whispered to his father. At each rotation of the wheel, the brace on his left leg caught in the front wheel. Papa shifted his foot further.

"I'll put a shield on the sides to keep them braces from catchin'," he told his son.

The shields did keep the braces from catching in the wheel, but they didn't make Jerome's legs turn the wheels of the cycle. He spent every afternoon after school sitting and trying to rock his cycle, but he never

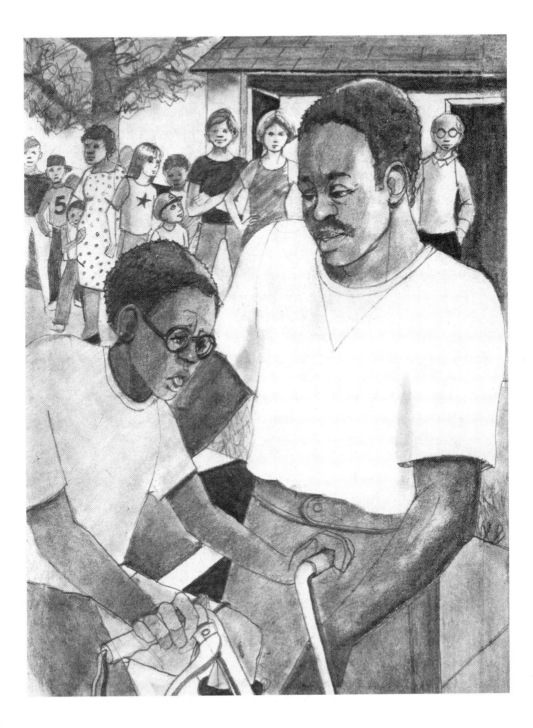

moved. Sometimes kids came along and pulled or
pushed him.

He had been able to get around by himself in
the wheelchair, but now he often got stranded on
his cycle. The kids would go in and leave him
around the corner or down the street and he
couldn't follow them. When dinner time came,
Mama or Tilly had to go looking for him. Mama
now added *contrary* to *ungrateful* when she
fussed at him.

And then something exciting happened. One
day he was turning the handlebars, weaving back
and forth, as some boys ran behind pushing him.
One sharp turn and the red cycle fell over. Mama
fussed about the bump on his forehead and his
scraped knee, but he felt happy and victorious.

"Yook, Papa," he called later when Papa
came in from work. "Uh gohh Band-Aid. Uh
busted muh knee."

He had calluses on his knees and hands from
crawling, but he never had a good hurt knee before.
Now he had joined all those other kids who got
to wear Band-Aids on their knees. Somehow
it made him feel he was really learning to ride.
Other kids fell off bicycles when they were
learning to ride, and he had fallen too. That night
he thought and thought and came up with a plan.

"Eh, Tilly," he called the next day. "Take
muh up by alley where slants to da strrrr-eet."

"Trucks come in the alley by the factory,
Jerome. You gotta stay on the sidewalk," Tilly
told him.

"Buttt Tilly, yuh be wid muh," he begged. "I cann-nn rrr-ride dere."

So Tilly pulled him along the block, not telling anyone where they were going. When they reached the alley, she sat in the uncut grass and chickweed watching for cars and reading a book. She enjoyed the peace and quiet. No one was around, so Jerome could grunt and sway all he needed, trying to pedal.

Three weeks passed and school was out. Every morning Tilly and Jerome went on their secret trip for a couple of hours. When Mama asked them where they went all morning, Jerome said, "Uh beennn near."

Mama accepted the fact that he stayed close, but Gordon could hardly wait to tell Papa that evening.

"Papa, Jerome say he drink beer and Mama didn't tell him nothing!"

Soon Jerome could shake the cycle enough on the slope so that his right leg got down fast enough for the left leg to reach the top of its pedal. Then he could grunt the stiff left leg down. He pedaled, but not always. He never could be sure. The dream of success was becoming a nightmare. He felt foolish and silly, not being able to depend on his rotten old legs.

"Tilly donnn' tellll," he begged. Every day they went to the alley. Tilly pulled the cycle out of the way when trucks came up to the factory, then she put her brother back on the slope and sat yawning, chin in hands, watching him struggle

with the red cycle. What was simple for a three-year-old was hard for her eleven-year-old brother!

Sometimes she wished he were somebody else's brother; sometimes she almost hated him, he was so stubborn and mean. Her head got all confused when Jerome was mean, and she often felt she didn't love him at all, but she stuck by him all the time.

By July he could ride down the slant, but he fought and struggled to ride up. Soon his legs moved one after the other, and he was riding. Some days Jerome nearly burst with triumph and Tilly wanted to tell Mama and Papa right away. But other days there was only failure. On those days his legs wouldn't push as he wished; in fact, they wouldn't move at all. He had nightmares about his legs not working when he tried to show Mama. In his dreams, Mama and Papa were watching and his legs wouldn't budge. His legs must learn to move one after the other all the time. He knew it wouldn't be easy and he was fighting hard. Gradually he became more sure of being able to pedal; his legs worked more often than they didn't.

In August smothering heat arrived, but Jerome forced his legs to move in spite of the sweat pouring off him. Besides Tilly, no one else knew how hard he was trying.

At home Mama was afraid to hope; it broke her heart to watch him sit still out front on that red cycle. Papa was afraid not to hope.

By then the kids on the block had decided that Jerome would never ride. He had been fun the way he was; if only he would be satisfied with himself. What was so important about riding that cycle?

The summer before, he had played baseball with the other kids and Tommy usually ran bases for him. But this summer he tripped Tommy and made his nose bleed. Then David ran his bases one day and Jerome threw a stone at him and David needed an ice pack. Now all Jerome did was sit alone on the big red cycle. The kids thought he was mean and they stopped playing with him. Why did he want that big cycle anyway?

But Jerome had his dream and he had chosen it carefully. It was something he could do, it was possible, and he would do it. It was one thing he would get to do all by himself. Tilly, it was true, brought him to the slanted drive, but *he* was the one fighting his legs to ride. He'd show Tommy and David and all the kids—he'd even show Tilly, because there was something secret he was practicing late at night all by himself.

By the end of August he could hardly wait to show off. As he became sure of himself, the perfect occasion came up. The neighbors planned a block party for Labor Day weekend.

That Saturday morning police closed the street at both ends, and teen-agers decorated trees with yellow crepe-paper banners. Neighbors held brightly colored balloons, and marching music filled the air. Everyone was dressed in cool, colorful clothes for the hot summer day.

In the morning there was a pet parade, then games with water-filled balloons. Artists of all ages drew pictures on the sidewalk with colored chalk. In the afternoon there was a program of local talent.

David played drums, Liza sang a funny song, and another girl arranged a mushroom dance with five little girls. Jerome knew that Tilly had put his name next on the program.

For the mushroom dance the little girls held umbrellas covered with brown paper. Everyone liked the silly twirling dance, and when they finished, Mrs. Mullarkey called out, "And next on our program is Jerome Johnson who will, who will . . . Jerome Johnson, folks!"

Everyone clapped politely. Then there was an eerie quiet. Adults and kids looked at one another to see if anyone knew what was going to happen. What was he going to do?

Tilly pulled her brother out into the street at the end of the block, and left him sitting on the shiny orange-red cycle. Her heart was pounding and she lowered her head and stuck her hands in her jean pockets as she strolled away from him. He was on his own.

Mama folded her arms to calm herself; Papa sat down on the curb because his knees grew weak. Liza hugged Gordon and waited. Gordon wondered if his brother would go to the moon now.

Jerome, frowning and gritting his teeth, struggled for what seemed like hours to get his legs moving. After two long minutes, slowly but firmly, he began pedaling—gripping the handles and leaning forward as though he were speeding along. There was no wind whipping in his face, but that didn't matter. He was riding his cycle himself; he was riding. That was all he could think.

The neighbors murmured and nodded to each other. Mrs. Mullarkey forgot she was holding the loudspeaker and blew her nose. The noise made everyone giggle nervously.

His progress down the street was slow, deliberate, and strangely rhythmic. People could hardly wait to applaud and, as he neared the end, clapping burst forth and the kids cheered, but he remained calm and cool.

"O.K.," he muttered to himself, "wid Tilly's help Uh learnnnn tuh ride. But nnnnnn-now Uh really show um."

He stopped in the middle of the street, opened the seat belt, and bowed with a flourish to the people on his right. When he bowed, he made sure he slipped his right foot out of the pedal strap. He bowed and waved to the people clapping on his left and slipped his left foot out of the pedal strap just as he had planned. His hands trembled.

Tilly wondered why he had stopped in the middle. She started toward him, but he stopped her with an icy scowl. Papa stood up, but Jerome frowned at him too.

Mama muttered, "Lordy, ain't enough he can ride, that silly boy gonna crawl off in the middle of the street."

The neighbors got quiet again.

Carefully Jerome slid his right leg around and off the cycle. He stood crouched on both feet, his knees and hips bent under his weight. He was grateful for the braces that kept his feet flat on the ground. At night when he had practiced this with his braces off, he stood on his toes.

He heard himself saying, "Uh wannn-na tank evv-body help muh, 'pecially muh sister Tilly, and muh Papa, and muh Mama." He nodded at Mama—he had said thank you and it didn't stick in his throat this time. There was a mild sprinkling of applause.

Then, while eighty people held their breath, he let go of the cycle. His arms wavered at his sides, balancing him. His head was high, his chin jutted forward. In spite of his eyeglasses everybody and everything was blurred.

He slid his stiff left leg forward, feet and knees twisted in; then he stepped jerkily off on his right foot. He dragged his left leg, stepped with his right. Deliberate, slow, arms waving in the air, one leg after the other, Jerome Johnson walked. It was stiff and clumsy walking, with twisted legs, but these were his first steps, practiced late at night.

Before he reached his wheelchair, he fell to the street. No one moved toward him. Clapping and cheering could be heard for five blocks. It was almost like thunder in the sky. His dream had come true.

He didn't try to get to his feet again, he crawled to his wheelchair. He'd work on walking with his physical therapist now that it wasn't a secret anymore. Now that he'd shown them how much he could do all by himself.

Mama was thanking the Lord, Papa cried and didn't care who saw him. Liza and Gordon were staring with mouths hanging open. For Gordon, his brother's going to the moon had seemed a simple thing; his brother's walking was far more wonderful.

Tilly rolled on the grass, laughing and crying and hugging herself for joy. Her tough, stubborn little brother had learned to ride a cycle and had taught himself to walk.

Jerome saw Tommy and David among the neighbors. Maybe he'd play some baseball with them. After all, he could walk now. Maybe next summer he would be running—even running his own bases.

Maybe he'd even . . .

Jerome was dreaming again.

WHY *RIDE THE RED CYCLE* IS IMPORTANT TO ME

Harriette Gillem Robinet

by Harriette Gillem Robinet

When my husband and I learned that our baby son Jonathan had cerebral palsy, we took him for medical help. At clinics we met other disabled children: a five-year-old girl crippled after a viral infection, a twelve-year-old boy who rode bicycles his father adapted for him.

At home we always read to our children. I wanted to read to them about a boy like Jonathan, but I discovered that there were no books about disabilities and courage. I decided to write a story of

courage concerning a child and a red tricycle. Jonathan was a year old when I wrote *Ride the Red Cycle*.

For ten years I mailed *Ride the Red Cycle* to publishers. Over twenty-five publishers rejected it. They didn't think anyone would want to read a book about a disabled child. And they didn't think the character Jerome seemed real.

When our son was eleven, his bad temper led him to beat up a classmate in school. It made me look again at my character Jerome in *Ride the Red Cycle*. Our son was full of courage, learning to walk time and again after four painful operations on his legs. He was also stubborn, insisting on doing things his way.

I realized that brave, disabled children are often stubborn and mean, and that Jerome was too sweet a character.

That year librarians decided they needed books about disabled children. The time was right. I rewrote my story and made Jerome stubborn and mean. The next publisher I sent it to bought the story and made it into a book.

Our beloved Jonathan is now in his twenties and lives on his own. He attended a community college and is a whiz at computers. He is still brave and still stubborn.

Young and old, with all our strengths and weaknesses, we must dream dreams and keep struggling until we fulfill them.

THINKING ABOUT IT

1 What did you live through with Jerome before you read the sentence "His dream had come true"?

2 What will happen next? Use the information from the story to predict what may happen later in Jerome's life.

3 Everyone has difficulty doing *something*. What task that you really want to learn to do well is difficult for you? How do you hope to succeed?

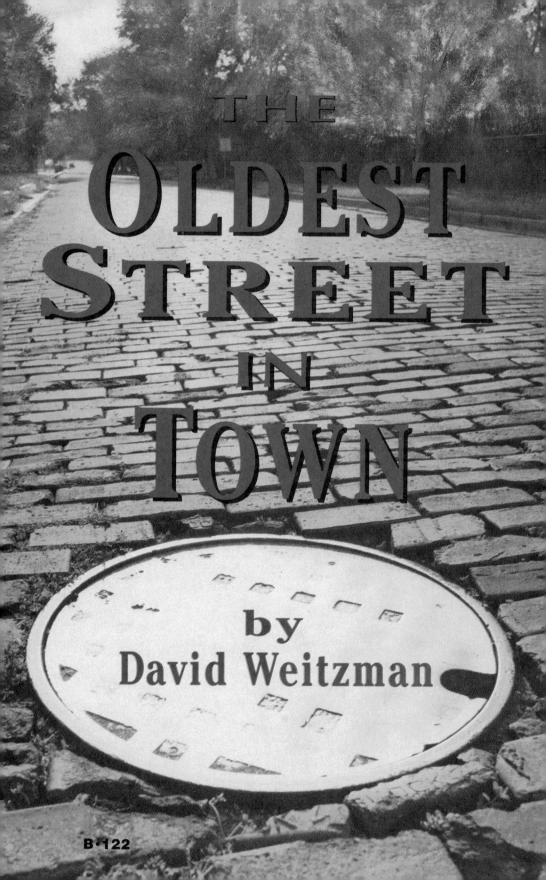

THE OLDEST STREET IN TOWN

by
David Weitzman

B·122

Does your town
have a Main
Street, a Center
Street, a First Avenue, or
an "A" Street? If it does,
I'll bet it's the oldest-
looking street in town.
And, if you were to look
closely for dates on the
cornerstones and arches
along that street, you'd
find that it's lined with
some of the first buildings
ever built in your city.

Say, come to think of it,
why have those streets got
names like that when they're
so far off the beaten path?
I hardly ever go there.

You don't, and chances
are they're not the main
street, center street, or
first avenue any more. But
they once were.

The city council may have
already made plans to tear
down the old part of town;
it's so dingy, so colorless
compared to the new,
thriving downtown. No
doubt there are already
empty lots between the old
buildings, filled with the
broken bricks and rubble
of a once colorful life.
So before it's too late,
take a walk down Main
Street, and take a stroll into
the past.

Here on Main Street you can close your eyes and imagine the sounds: old cars put-putting and beep-beeping their way down streets filled with the noise of horses, clanging trolley cars, and clattering carts. On the sidewalks there are women in long skirts and high-top shoes, and a bustle of workers in overalls, and clerks in stiff collars and vests. Here you can begin to understand something of your town's history if you watch carefully for the small but unmistakable bits of the past . . . .

cobblestones showing through the pavement

glimpses of old trolley tracks

an iron drinking trough for horses with a little bubbly fountain for people

elaborate cast-iron lampposts

gas lamps jutting out from old brick building fronts

little fire hydrants

This is where it all began. Perhaps, being here, you can discover by yourself how your town began.

Like people, towns have a birth, a youth, maturity, and old age. Like people, towns also have personalities; they are serious, and they laugh. Cared for, they flourish; unloved and neglected, they perish.

But unlike people, who sort of grow in every direction at once, towns tend to start at one point and grow outward.

There are any number of ways a town gets started. Lots of towns have railroad tracks running right through them. And there, just off Main Street, is the old yellow and brown station calling our attention to its role in the town's growth. It's probably very quiet now. Go take a look inside its windows and let your imagination take you back into the past . . . .

Seventy or a hundred years ago that station stood alone, nothing for miles around; alone, that is, until the cattle drives began and thousands of head of cattle arrived for shipment by train to the slaughterhouses in the big city.

Then, over the years, things changed. Bigger cattle pens were built. Hotels and saloons popped up, as did general stores, banks, firms that bought and sold cattle, and, of course, houses for all the people running these businesses.

Soon manufacturers arrived to take advantage of the access to the railroad, and the town gradually became a large transportation and manufacturing center, with more houses and stores.

So, the city grows out and away from its reason for being—the railroad tracks.

Other cities began as transportation centers too, but of a different kind— ships and shipping. These towns grew around the wharfs and docks along rivers, or around natural harbors on the sea coast.

Even today, you can see the pattern of growth of river and seaport towns when you walk away from the port's docks and notice how the city becomes newer and newer the farther out you get.

And still another kind of
city started at a crossroads.
It began with a gas station,
then a restaurant and bus
stop, then a general store,

and then—when a lot of
the people who got off the
buses didn't get back
on—some houses,
churches, and schools.

And there are still other kinds of beginnings for cities. There are university towns, manufacturing cities, county seats, state capitals, and mining towns. More recently, whole cities have grown around recreation areas and retirement communities.

Now, does that give you any ideas on how your town began and why?

It may be a little difficult to tell just what the original purpose of your city was; things have changed so much. (For example, because railroads are not as important as they used to be, many railroad towns may have changed colors and become manufacturing towns.)

If you don't come up with an answer right away, there are some suggestions coming up for finding out more about the history of where you live, preserving some of that past, and most important, enjoying being where you are.

Hanging around old town

And while you're thinking about how it all began, there's lots to look at, and do. The older parts of cities are disappearing now, being eaten up by bulldozers and the mad dash into the future. In a few years just about the only thing left in your city or town that is as much as fifty or a hundred years old may be what's in your memory. (There are groups of people around who, like you, have become interested in the history of their community and are trying to save it.)

One way to keep that memory vivid is to spend some time in the old part of town. While you're at it you can "collect" some bits and pieces of the past that interest you, and keep them alive. The first thing you can do is to make an Old Town map. It won't be a fancy map, but one you can write all over and keep notes on.

Before you leave home make sure you've got either a notepad or a clipboard with some paper in it, and a pencil, and your camera—don't forget your camera.

Where to start

If after reading that little description of how towns got started you've made a guess about yours, then start investigating that hunch. Begin at the railroad tracks (where they cross Main Street), or at the wharf, or maybe at a large meat processing plant, or stockyards. (Don't worry if your hunch turns out not to be quite right; you'll have fun anyway.)

What to do

When you get to what you think is the oldest part of town, try to make a rough map as you go along. Your first notes might look like this:

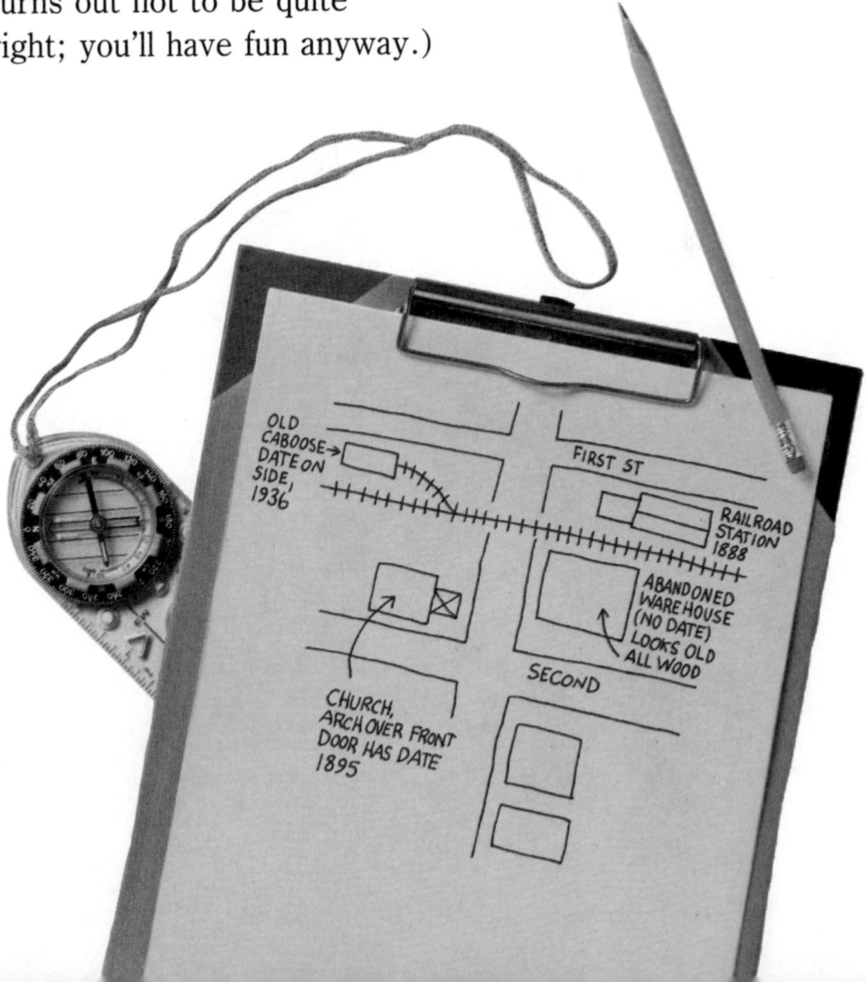

OLD CABOOSE→ DATE ON SIDE, 1936

FIRST ST

RAILROAD STATION 1888

ABANDONED WAREHOUSE (NO DATE) LOOKS OLD ALL WOOD

SECOND

CHURCH, ARCH OVER FRONT DOOR HAS DATE 1895

After you've walked for a while up and down a couple of blocks of Main Street, spend some time on First and Second Streets. All the time you're walking, keep on the lookout for some of these clues:

Dates engraved on cornerstones, in stone around doors or on the sides of buildings, or on metal plaques.

Old sidewalks. Often you'll find that the name of the company that put down the sidewalk is stamped into the wet cement in a few places (usually at the corner) and these stamps are often dated. Sometimes there are metal plates set into the cement.

Cast-iron building fronts, lampposts, fire hydrants, manhole covers, railings, and fences with dates cast into them.

Old signs on the sides of buildings. What kinds of businesses are here? Industries? Warehouses? Lumber yards? Is there more of one kind of business than others? Write down some of the names you see on the old signs. Was the town once mostly of one nationality?

And clues at the railroad station. Are there maps painted on the sides of the old freight cars or at the railroad station that show the old routes? Are there any special structures around that give clues to what the trains carried in and out of town (storage tanks, grain silos, saw mills)?

Do you suppose you've really found the oldest part of the city, all by yourself?

Well, most likely you have, but if you want to check up on how you're doing there are several ways of finding out just how good a guesser you are.

Go to the city or county clerk's office (usually in the city or county office building) and ask to see the earliest map of the city they have. The clerk is there to serve the public—including amateur historians—and should be very helpful. Ask how you can get a copy of the map.

Visit your town's main library and ask the librarian where the local history section is. Ask if there are any histories of the community which might be in a special collection.

Go to a realtor's office, one which has been around for a long time. Ask if they have any old maps of the city and if you can have a copy or get one made. (Sometimes they have old photographs too.)

Tell people what you're doing. They'll get interested too and give you enough information and suggestions for dozens of backyard history projects.

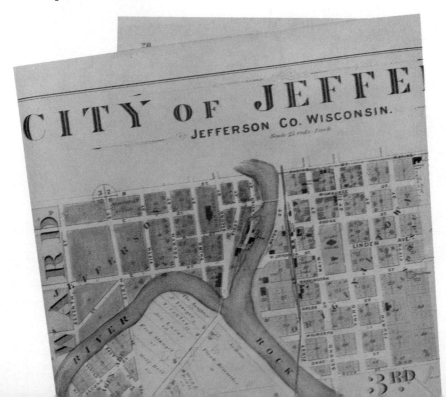

PULLING IT ALL TOGETHER

1 Many people think of particular places as they read *The Oldest Street in Town*. Tell what you thought about as you read the article.

2 All the characters learned something new in *The World Is Round Just Like an Orange*. Which character do you think learned the most important thing? What did the person learn? Why was it important?

3 You are the editor of *The World Is Round Just Like an Orange*. Take out one of the selections in this book and replace it with another story with the same theme or idea. Which story or article will you replace? What will you replace it with?

BOOKS TO ENJOY

Cars and How They Go
by Joanna Cole
Cars aren't so hard to figure out! This book makes it fun to know about cars and engines.

In the Year of the Boar and Jackie Robinson
by Bette Bao Lord
Sixth Cousin Wong needs an American name. Uncle Sam doesn't sound quite right, so she settles for Shirley Temple. Now she's ready for adventure in her new home.

Conquista!
by Clyde Robert Bulla and Michael Syson
Travel back in time to the 1500s. A young boy comes across one of the first horses brought to North America. What is this magical creature? Is it friend or foe? Learning how to ride the horse becomes one of the most important things Little Wolf learns to do.

Adventures in Your National Parks
National Geographic Society
Go rafting, rock climbing, hiking, and paddling with students your age as they explore some of our national parks.

Juma and the Magic Jinn

by Joy Anderson
illustrations by Charles Mikolaycak
Juma would rather draw and write poems than learn his sums in school. Then comes a magical creature, who lives in his mother's jinn jar.

Secrets of a Wildlife Watcher

by Jim Arnosky
The best way to learn is by doing: if you want to learn about animals, go out and study them. This book will help you set up a wildlife watch.

Maxie, Rosie and Earl—Partners in Grime

by Barbara Park
What could a tattletale, the class brain, and a nervous newcomer possibly have in common? Nothing much, until the three find themselves trapped in the same school dumpster.

Top Secret

by John Reynolds Gardiner
Allen wants his science project to win the silver trophy award. He wants to discover the secret of human photosynthesis—how to turn people into plants. Then he turns green and begins to sprout roots.

LITERARY TERMS

Biography

A **biography** is the history of a person's life. "Yani's Monkeys" is a biography. It gives you information about Wang Yani's life and her artwork.

Character

An author can show what a character is like by the way the character behaves. As you observe Cricket Kaufman in "The Imperfect/ Perfect Book Report," you begin to understand what she is like and how she begins to change.

Expository nonfiction

Expository writing explains something about a subject. A science article about black holes or about simple machines is expository. "The Oldest Street in Town" is expository nonfiction.

Folk tale

Folk tales are stories handed down through the generations by word of mouth. At some point along the way, many folk tales are written down so that more people can enjoy them. The

grandfather in "Pop Goes the Popcorn" tells his grandson a folk tale.

Plot

Sometimes the plot of a story develops because a character is struggling with some problem within himself. This happens in "Cheating" when the boy worries and worries until he finally admits he has cheated on a test. The action in *Ride the Red Cycle* unfolds because Jerome is struggling with his own problems. He wants to be like other boys and so he learns first to ride a tricycle and then to walk. The things he does to try to overcome his problems make up the plot of the book.

Realistic Fiction

In **realistic fiction,** the characters, setting, and plot seem true to life. Modern realistic fictional stories

could be happening now to someone like you or your friends. "Cheating" is a story that could happen to someone in your class. Perhaps "The Disaster" could too.

Theme

The **theme,** an underlying message or meaning of a story, is what holds the story together. All through *Ride the Red Cycle,* Jerome shows that he is brave and stubborn enough to try new things even though he fails at first. How courage and determination can overcome obstacles is one of the themes of the book.

GLOSSARY

Vocabulary from your selections

ac·ci·dent (ak′sə dənt),
1 something harmful or unlucky that happens unexpectedly.
2 something that happens without being planned or known in advance. *noun.*

ad·just (ə just′), 1 to arrange; set just right; change to make fit. 2 to get used to; become accustomed to. *verb.*

arch (ärch), 1 a curved structure that bears the weight of the material above it. Arches often form the tops of doors, windows, and gateways. 2 to bend into an arch; curve. 1 *noun, plural* **arch·es;** 2 *verb.*

arch (definition 1)—The courtyard is ringed by **arches**.

as·sign·ment (ə sīn′mənt),
1 something assigned: *an arithmetic assignment* 2 an assigning or a being assigned: *room assignments. noun.*

bar·ren (bar′ən), 1 not able to bear seeds, fruit, or young. 2 not able to produce much: *a barren desert. adjective.*

barren (definition 2)—Mars has a **barren** landscape.

cheat (chēt), 1 to deceive or trick; do business or play in a way that is not honest. 2 a person who is not honest and does things to deceive and trick others. 1 *verb,* 2 *noun.*

cinch (sinch), 1 a strong strap for fastening a saddle or pack on a horse. 2 to fasten on with a cinch; bind firmly. 3 something sure and easy: *It's a cinch to ride a bike once you know how.* 1,3 *noun, plural* **cinch·es;** 2 *verb.*

con·fide (kən fīd′), to show trust by telling secrets: *She always confided in her friend. verb,* **con·fides, con·fid·ed, con·fid·ing.**

con·grat·u·late (kən grach′ə lāt), to express pleasure at the happiness or good fortune of. *verb,* **con·grat·u·lates, con·grat·u·lat·ed, con·grat·u·lat·ing.**

con·tra·ry (kon′trer ē *for 1 and 2;* kən trer′ē *for 3*), **1** opposed; opposite; completely different: *Her taste in music is contrary to mine.* **2** the opposite: *After promising to come early, she did the contrary and came late.* **3** opposing others; stubborn: *The contrary boy often refused to do what was suggested.* 1,3 *adjective,* 2 *noun.*

coun·se·lor (koun′sə lər), **1** a person who gives advice; adviser: *The counselor at school helps us decide which courses to take.* **2** a lawyer. **3** an instructor or leader in a summer camp. *noun.*

crest·fall·en (krest′fô′lən), dejected; discouraged: *The students who had failed the test were crestfallen. adjective.*

crit·i·cize (krit′ə sīz), **1** to blame; find fault with. **2** to judge or speak as a critic: *The teacher criticized her students' writing with helpful comments. verb,* **crit·i·ciz·es, crit·i·cized, crit·i·ciz·ing.**

dem·on·strate (dem′ən strāt), **1** to show clearly; prove: *The pianist demonstrated her musical skill.* **2** to explain by the use of examples. **3** to show or make known the quality of. **4** to take part in a parade or meeting to protest or to make demands. *verb,* **dem·on·strates, dem·on·strat·ed, dem·on·strat·ing.**

eer·ie (ir′ē), strange; weird; causing fear: *A dark, eerie old house stood at the end of the driveway. adjective,* **eer·i·er, eer·i·est.**

e·lab·or·ate (i lab′ər it *for 1;* i lab′ə rāt′ *for 2*), **1** worked out with great care; having many details; complicated: *They made elaborate plans for the birthday party.* **2** to give added details; say or write more: *The witness was asked to elaborate on one of his statements.* 1 *adjective,* 2 *verb,* **e·lab·or·ates, e·lab·or·at·ed, e·lab·or·at·ing.**

en·grave (en grāv′), **1** to carve in; carve in an artistic way: *The jeweler engraved the boy's initials on the back of the watch.* **2** to cut a picture, design, or map in lines on wood, stone, metal, or glass plates for printing. *verb,* **en·graves, en·graved, en·grav·ing.**

engrave (definition 1)—A worker **engraves** a design on a saxophone.

en·hance (en hans′), to add to; make greater: *A new roof or a paint job enhances the value of a house. verb,* **en·hanc·es, en·hanced, en·hanc·ing.**

en·vi·ron·ment (en vī′rən mənt), all of the surroundings that influence the growth, development, and well-being of a living thing: *A plant will often grow differently in a different environment. noun.*

a hat	o hot	ch child	ə stands for:
ā age	ō open	ng long	a in about
ä far	ô order	sh she	e in taken
e let	oi oil	th thin	i in pencil
ē equal	ou out	₮ₕ then	o in lemon
ėr term	u cup	zh measure	u in circus
i it	ů put		
ī ice	ü rule		

ex·pand (ek spand′), to spread out; open out; unfold; swell; make or grow larger: *A balloon expands when it is blown up. A bird expands its wings before flying.* verb.

flour·ish (flėr′ish), **1** to grow or develop with vigor; do well; thrive. *Their newspaper business grew and flourished.* **2** to wave in the air. **3** a waving about in the air: *The magician removed his cape with a flourish.* *1,2 verb,* *3 noun, plural* **flour·ish·es.**

friend·ship (frend′ship), **1** the condition of being friends: *Our friendship lasted for many years.* **2** friendly feeling or behavior; friendliness: *We tried to be helpful and show friendship to the foreign visitors.* noun.

fur·nace (fėr′nis), an enclosed space to make a very hot fire in. Furnaces are used to heat buildings, melt metals, and make glass. *noun.*

gift·ed (gif′tid), very able; having special ability: *a gifted musician.* *adjective.*

im·per·fect (im pėr′fikt), not perfect; having some defect or fault. *adjective.*

im·press (im pres′), **1** to have a strong effect on the mind or feelings of: *We were impressed with the courage of the twins who saved their brother from the burning house.* **2** to fix in the mind: *I repeated the words to impress them in my memory. verb.*

im·prove (im prüv′), to make or become better: *Try to improve your spelling. His health is improving. verb,* **im·proves,** **im·proved, im·prov·ing.**

in·fec·tion (in fek′shən), **1** a causing of disease in people and other living things by bringing into contact with germs. **2** a disease caused in this manner, especially one that can spread from one person to another. *noun.*

ma·tur·i·ty (mə chur′ə tē, mə tur′ə tē, *or* mə tyur′ə tē), **1** a ripeness; full development: *The frost struck before the peaches could reach maturity.* **2** the condition of being mature: *He reached maturity at an early age. noun.*

med·i·ta·tion (med′ə tā′shən), any quiet thought, especially about serious things. *noun.*

mem·o·rize (mem′ə rīz′), to commit to memory; learn by heart. *verb,* **mem·o·riz·es,** **mem·o·rized, mem·o·riz·ing.**

mois·ture (mois′chər), a slight wetness; water or other liquid spread in very small drops in the air or on a surface. Dew is moisture that collects at night on the grass.

naugh·ty (nô′tē), bad; not behaving well: *The naughty child hit the baby. adjective,* **naugh·ti·er, naugh·ti·est.**

pan·ick·y (pan′ə kē), **1** caused by panic: *panicky haste.* **2** feeling panic; liable to panic: *When fire broke out in the theater, the audience became panicky.* *adjective.*

per·ish (per′ish), to be destroyed; die: *They perished in the fire. verb.*